The Britannica Guide to Islam

ISLAMIC LITERATURE

Edited by Lucy Sackett Smith

Britannica Educational Publishing
in association with
ROSEN
Educational Services

Published in 2018 by Britannica Educational Publishing (a trademark of Encyclopædia Britannica, Inc.) in association with The Rosen Publishing Group, Inc.
29 East 21st Street, New York, NY 10010

Distributed exclusively by Rosen Publishing.
To see additional Britannica Educational Publishing titles, go to rosenpublishing.com.

First Edition

Britannica Educational Publishing
J.E. Luebering: Executive Director, Core Editorial
Andrea R. Field: Managing Editor, Compton's by Britannica

Rosen Publishing
Amelie von Zumbusch: Editor
Nelson Sá: Art Director
Brian Garvey: Series Designer
Tahara Anderson: Book Layout
Cindy Reiman: Photography Manager
Nicole DiMella: Photo Researcher

Library of Congress Cataloging-in-Publication Data

Names: Smith, Lucy Sackett, editor.
Title: Islamic literature / [editor] Lucy Sackett Smith.
Description: New York, NY : Britannica Educational Publishing, 2018. | Series: The Britannica guide to Islam | Includes bibliographical references and index.
Identifiers: LCCN 2016053717 | ISBN 9781680486155 (library bound : alk. paper)
Subjects: LCSH: Islamic literature—History and criticism. | Arabic literature—History and criticism. | Persian literature—History and criticism. | Turkish literature—History and criticism.
Classification: LCC PJ807 .I85 2018 | DDC 809/.8921297—dc23
LC record available at https://lccn.loc.gov/2016053717

Manufactured in China

Photo credits: Cover, p. 1 Bertrand Guay/AFP/Getty Images; p. 9 The Walters Art Museum/W.626.289A/CC0; p. 13 Shinji Shumeikai Discretionary Fund/AC1999.158.1/www.lacma.org; p. 15 The Nasli M. Heeramaneck Collection, gift of Joan Palevsky/M.73.5.18/www.lacma.org; pp. 26, 102 Heritage Images/Hulton Archive/Getty Images; pp. 29, 38 Pictures from History/Bridgeman Images; p. 33 Lynn Abercrombie; p. 34 Everett - Art/Shutterstock.com; p. 41 © British Library Board/Robana/Art Resource, NY; p. 43 Bloomberg/Getty Images; p. 46 Joeri De Rocker/Alamy Stock Photo; pp. 49, 64 Universal History Archive/Universal Images Group/Getty Images; p. 53 Bibliotheque de la Faculte de Medecine, Paris, France/Archives Charmet/Bridgeman Images; p. 56 Encyclopædia Britannica, Inc.; p. 60 Laurie Noble/Photolibrary/Getty Images; p. 62 The Nasli M. Heeramaneck Collection, gift of Joan Palevsky-/M.73.5.410/www.lacma.org; p. 67 DEA/J. E. Bulloz/De Agostini Picture Library/Getty Images; p. 69 Private Collection/Bridgeman Images; p. 72 The Walters Art Museum/W.626.94B/CC0; p. 75 Reproduced by permission of the British Library; p. 80 Courtesy of the trustees of the British Museum, photograph, J.R. Freeman & Co. Ltd.; p. 82 Freer Gallery of Art, Smithsonian Institution, USA/Bridgeman Images; p. 89 The Granger Collection, New York; p. 93 Gift of The Walter Foundation/M.91.348.1/www.lacma.org; p. 96 Henry Guttmann/Hulton Royals Collection/Getty Images; p. 106 Courtesy www.eltaher.org; p. 112 Keystone/Hulton Archive/Getty Images; p. 116 © SZ Photo/Bridgeman Images; p. 120 Thomas Hartwell/The LIFE Images Collection/Getty Images; back cover, pp. 3–7 background design javarman/Shutterstock.com; interior pages border design Azat1976/Shutterstock.com.

CONTENTS

CHAPTER 5

INTRODUCTION

It would be almost impossible to make an exhaustive survey of Islamic literatures. There are so many works, of which hundreds of thousands are available only in manuscript, that even a very large team of scholars could scarcely master a single branch of the subject. On top of that, Islamic literatures exist over a vast geographical and linguistic area. This happened because they were produced wherever the Muslims went, pushing out from their heartland in Arabia through the countries of the Middle East as far as Spain, North Africa, and, eventually, West Africa. Persia (now Iran) is a major centre of Islam, along with the neighbouring areas that came under Persian influence, including Turkey and the Turkic-speaking peoples of Central Asia. Many Indian languages have a literature that focuses almost exclusively on Islamic literary subjects. There is an Islamic content in the literature of Malaysia and in that of some East African languages, including Swahili. In many cases, however, the Islamic content proper is restricted to religious works—mystical treatises, books on Islamic law and its implementation, historical works praising the heroic deeds and miraculous adventures of earlier Muslim rulers and saints, or devotional works in honour of the Prophet Muhammad.

The vast majority of Arabic writings are scholarly. The same, indeed, is true of the other languages in which Islamic literature has been written. There are superb historically important translations made by medieval scholars from Greek into Arabic. There are historical works, as well as a range of religiously inspired works. There are books on grammar, style, ethics, and philosophy. All have helped to shape the spirit of Islamic literature in general, and it is often difficult to draw a line between such works of "scholarship" and works of "literature" in the narrower sense of that term. Even a strictly theological commentary can bring about a deeper understanding of some problem of aesthetics. A work of history composed in florid and artistic language would certainly be regarded by its author as a work of art as well as of scholarship, whereas the grammarian would be equally sure that his keen insights into the structure of Arabic grammar were of the utmost importance in preserving that literary beauty in which Arabs and non-Arabs alike took pride.

In this treatment of Islamic literatures, however, the definition of "literature" is restricted to poetry and literary prose, whether popular or courtly in inspiration. Other categories of writing will be dealt with briefly if these shed light on some particular aspect of literature.

Jalāl al-Dīn Rūmī was a Sufi mystic and one of the greatest poets in Islamic literature. This manuscript page comes from a copy of his *Mas̆navī*, a collection of poems.

In its earliest days, the poetry of the Arabs consisted of praise and satirical poems thought to be full of magical qualities. The strict rules of the outward form of the poems (monorhyme, complicated metre) even in pre-Islamic times led to a certain formalism and encouraged imitation. Another early poetic form was the elegy, as noted in the work of the Arab female poet al-Khansāʾ.

For the most part, however, Goethe's statement that the stories of *The Thousand and One Nights* have no goal in themselves shows his understanding of the character of Arabic belles lettres, contrasting them with the Islamic religion, which aims at "collecting and uniting people in order to achieve one high goal." Poets, on the other hand, rove around without any ethical purpose, according to the Qurʾān. For many pious Muslims, poetry was something suspect, opposed to the divine law, especially since it sang mostly of forbidden wine and of free love. The combination of music and poetry, as practiced in court circles and among the mystics, has always aroused the wrath of the lawyer divines who wield so much authority in Islamic communities. This opposition may partly explain why Islamic poetry and fine arts took refuge in a kind of unreal world, using fixed images that could be correctly interpreted only by those who were knowledgeable in the art.

The ambiguity of Persian poetry, which oscillates between the worldly, the divine, and often the political level, is typical of Islamic writings. Especially in Iran and the countries under its cultural influence, this kind of poetry formed the most important part of literature. Epic poetry of all kinds developed exclusively outside the Arabic-speaking countries; Western readers look in vain for an epical structure in such long poems (as in the case of the prose-romances of the Arabs). A similar characteristic even conditions innumerable historical works in Arabic, Persian, and Turkish, which, especially in classical times, contain much valuable information; only rarely does the historian or philosopher reach a comprehensive view. The accumulation of large amounts of material, which is carefully organized up to the present, seems typical of all branches of Islamic scholarship, from theology to natural sciences. There are many minute observations and descriptions but rarely a full view of the whole process. Later, especially in the Persian, Turkish, and Indo-Muslim areas, a tendency to stress the decorative elements of prose is evident, and the contents even of official chronicles are hidden behind a network of rhymed prose.

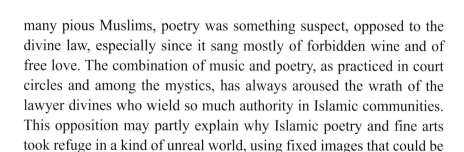

This tendency is illustrated in all branches of Islamic art: the lack of "architectural" formation. Instead, there is a kind of carpetlike pattern; the Arabic and Persian poem is, in general, judged not as a closed unity but rather according to the perfection of its individual verses. Its main object is less to convey a deep personal feeling than to perfect to the utmost the traditional rules and inherited metaphors, to which a new image may sometimes be added. Thus, the personality of the poet becomes visible primarily through the minimal changes of expression and rhythm and the application of certain preferred metaphors, just as the personality of the miniature painter can be detected by a careful observation of details, of his way of colouring a rock or deepening the shade of a turban. The same holds true for the arabesques, which were developed according to a strict ritual to a mathematical pattern and were refined until they reached a perfection of geometrically complicated figures, as in the dome of the Karatay Medrese in Konya (1251); it corresponds both to the most intricate lacelike Kūfic inscriptions around this dome and to the poetical style of Jalāl al-Dīn Rūmī, who wrote in that very place and during those years. His immortal mystical poems comprise thousands of variations on the central theme of love. The tile work of a Persian mosque, which combines different levels of arabesque work with different styles of writing, is reminiscent of the way Persian poetry combines at least two levels of reality. And a perfect harmony is reached in some of the miniature manuscripts of Iran, Muslim India, or Ottoman Turkey, which, in their lucid colours and fine details of execution, recall both the perfection of the calligraphy that surrounds them on delicate paper and the subtlety of the stories or poems that they accompany or illustrate.

Chapter 1

The Range of Islamic Literatures

Islamic literatures appear in a wide range of languages and in many different cultural environments. Nevertheless, to quote G. E. von Grunebaum's classic *Islam: Essays in the Nature and Growth of a Cultural Tradition*, their unity

> is safeguarded by the identity of the basic existential experience, by the identity of the fundamental intellectual interests, by the authoritativeness of certain principles of form and presentation, not to mention the kindred political and social organization within which those peoples aspire to live.

Arabic: Language of the Qur'ān

The area of Islamic culture extends from western Africa to Malaysia, Indonesia, and the Philippines, but its heartland is Arabia. The importance and special authority of the Arabic language has remained largely unquestioned after the spread of Islam. The Arabic poetry of pre-Islamic Arabia was seen for centuries to come as the standard model for all Islamic poetic achievement. It directly influenced literary forms in many non-Arab literatures. The Qur'ān, Islam's sacred scripture, is accepted by pious Muslims as God's uncreated word and is considered to be the highest manifestation of literary beauty. A

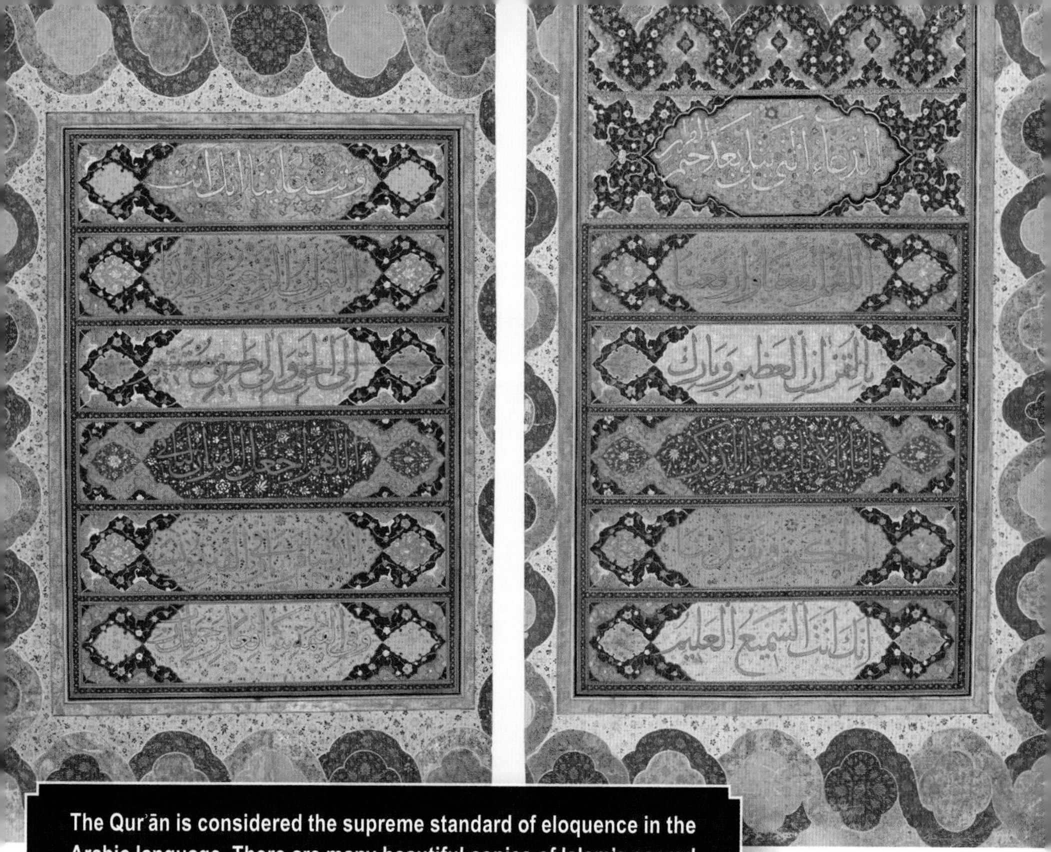

The Qurʾān is considered the supreme standard of eloquence in the Arabic language. There are many beautiful copies of Islam's sacred book. This one was made in Iran during the 16th century.

whole literature defended its inimitability (*iʿjāz*) and unsurpassable beauty. Because it was God's own word, the Qurʾān could not legitimately be translated into any other language. The study of at least some Arabic was therefore required of every Muslim. Arabic script was used by all those peoples who followed Islam, however much their own languages might differ in structure from Arabic. The Qurʾān became the textbook of the Muslims' entire philosophy of life. Theology, lexicography (the compiling of dictionaries), geography, historiography (the writing of history), and mysticism all grew out of a deep study of its form and content. Allusions to the holy book can be found even in the most secular works. Its imagery not unexpectedly permeates all Islamic poetry and prose.

Between the coming of Islam in the 7th century and the 11th century, a great deal of poetry and prose in Arabic was produced. For example, the literature of Spain and North Africa matured in perfect harmony with the classical ideals of the Muslim East, although its masters invented a few poetic forms unknown to classical Arabic poetry. In modern times North African Muslim literature—mainly from Algeria and Morocco—often uses French as a means of expression. This is because the tradition of Arabic writing was interrupted by the French occupation in the 19th century and has had to be built up afresh.

Persian

In 640 the Muslims entered Iran, and Persian influence on literary taste is apparent in Arabic literature from the mid-8th century onward. Many stories and tales were transmitted from, or through, Iran to the Arab world and often from there to western Europe. Soon Iran could boast a large literature in its own tongue. Persian literature was more varied in its forms and content than that written in classical Arabic. Although Persian adopted many of the formal rules of the Arabic language (including rhyme patterns), new genres, including epic poetry, were introduced from Iran. Lyric poetry (which is poetry expressing a poet's own feeling), elegant and supple, also reached its finest expression in the Persian language.

South Asian

Persian culture was by no means restricted to Iran itself. Northwestern India and what is now Pakistan became a centre of Islamic literature as early as the 11th century, with Delhi and Agra being of special importance. It was to remain a stronghold of Muslim cultural life, which soon also extended to the east (Bengal) and south (Deccan). Persian remained the official language of Muslim India until

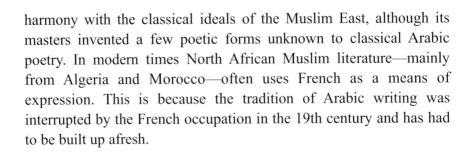

In the *Shāh-nāmeh*, the Persian national epic found its final and enduring form. Completed in 1010, this poem of nearly 60,000 verses is by the poet Ferdowsī.

1835, and not only its poetry but even its historiography was written in the high-flown manner that exemplified the Persian concept of fine style. Muslim India can further boast a fine heritage of Arabic poetry and prose (theological, philosophical, and mystical works).

At various times in its history the Indian subcontinent was ruled by princes of Turkish origin (indeed, the words "Turk" and "Muslim" became synonymous in some Indian languages). The princes surrounded themselves with a military aristocracy of mainly Turkish extraction, and a few poetical and prose works in Turkish were thus written at some Indian courts. In various regions of the subcontinent an extremely pleasing folk literature has flourished throughout the ages: Sindhi in the lower Indus Valley, for example, and Punjabi in the Punjab are languages rich in an emotional poetry that uses popular metres and forms. At the Indo-Iranian border the oldest fragments of the powerful Pashto poetry date from the Middle Ages. The neighbouring Balochi poetry consists largely of ballads and religious folk songs. All the peoples in this area have interpreted Islamic mysticism in their own simple, touching imagery. In the east of the subcontinent Bengali Muslims possess a large Islamic literary heritage, including religious epics from the 14th and 15th centuries and some lovely religious folk songs. The achievements of modern novelists and lyric poets from Bangladesh are impressive. As a result of the spread of Islam to the north in the 14th century, a number of classical themes in Islamic lore were elaborated in Kashmiri lyric and epic poetry. To the south an occasional piece of Islamic religious poetry can be found even in Tamil and Malayalam. Some fine Muslim short stories have been produced in modern Malayalam.

Urdu, now the chief literary language of Muslim India and Pakistan, borrowed heavily from Persian literature during its classical period in the 18th century. In many writings only the verbs are in Urdu, the rest consisting of Persian constructions and vocabulary, and the themes of traditional Urdu literature were often adapted from Persian. Modern Urdu prose, however, has freed itself almost completely from the past, whereas in poetry promising steps have been taken toward modernization of both forms and content.

Turkish and Turkic Languages

An elaborate "classical" style developed in Turkish after the 14th century, reaching its peak in the 17th. Like classical Urdu, it was heavily influenced by Persian in metrics and vocabulary. Many exponents of this "high" style came from the Balkan provinces of the Ottoman Empire. On the other hand, a rich and moving folk poetry in popular syllable-counting metres has always flourished among the Turkish population of Anatolia and Rumelia. The mystical songs of the poet Yunus Emre (died *c.* 1320) contributed greatly toward shaping this body of literature, which was preserved in the religious centres of the Sufi orders of Islam. From this folk tradition, as well as from Western literature, modern Turkish literature has derived a great deal of its inspiration.

A great deal of the Muslim literature of Central Asia is written in Turkic languages, which include Uzbek, Tatar, and Kyrgyz. Its main cultural centres (Samarkand, Bukhara, Fergana) became part of the Muslim empire after 711. Central Asia was an important centre of Islamic learning until the tsarist invasions in the 1870s, and the peoples of this region have produced a classical literature in Arabic. Many of the most famous Arabic and Persian scholars and poets writing in the heyday of Muslim influence were Central Asians by birth. Central Asians also possess a considerable literature of their own, consisting in large part of epics, folktales, and mystical "words of wisdom." The rules of prosody that hold for Arabic and Persian languages have been deliberately imposed on the Turkic languages on

Islamic Literatures and the West

Small fragments of Arabic literature have long been known in the West. There were cultural interrelations between Muslim Spain (which, like the Indus Valley, became part of the Muslim empire after 711) and its Christian neighbours, and this meant that many philosophical and scientific works filtered through to western Europe. It is also likely that the poetry of Muslim Spain influenced the growth of certain forms of Spanish and French troubadour poetry and provided an element, however distorted, for medieval Western romances and heroic tales.

Investigation of Eastern literatures by Western scholars did not begin until the 16th century in the Netherlands and England. First attempts toward an aesthetic understanding of Arabic and Persian poetry came even later: they were made by the British scholars of Fort William, Calcutta (now Kolkata), and by German pre-Romantics of the late 18th century. In the first half of the 19th century the publication of numerous translations of Eastern poetry, especially into German, began to interest some Europeans. The poetical translations from Arabic, Persian, and Sanskrit made by the German poet Friedrich Rückert can scarcely be surpassed, either in accuracy or in poetical mastery. The Persian poet Ḥāfeẓ became well known in German-speaking countries, thanks to Johann Wolfgang von Goethe's enchanting *West-östlicher Divan* (1819; "The Parliament of East and West;" Eng. trans. *Poems of the East and West*), a collection of self-consciously Persian-style poetry, which represented the first Western response to and appreciation of the character of Middle Eastern poetry by an acknowledged giant of European literature. An "Orientalizing style," which employed Arabo-Persian literary forms such as the *ghazal* (a short graceful poem with monorhyme), became fashionable at times in Germany. Later, Edward FitzGerald aroused new interest in Persian poetry with his free adaptations of Omar Khayyam's *robāʿīyyāt* (*The Rubáiyát of Omar Khayyám*, 1859). The fairy tales known as *The Thousand and One Nights*, first translated in 1704, provided abundant raw material for many a Western writer's play, novel, story, or poem about the Islamic East.

several occasions, notably by ʿAlī Shīr Navāʾī (died 1501), a master of Chagatai poetry and prose in Herāt, and by Bābur (died 1530), the first Mughal emperor in India. Tajik literature is basically Persian, both as it is written today in Tajikistan and as it existed in earlier forms, when it was indistinguishable from classical Persian. After the Russification of the country, and especially after the 1917 Revolution, a new literature emerged that was part and parcel of the former Soviet literature. The same can be said, by and large, about the literatures of other Muslim Turkic peoples of Central Asia.

OTHER LANGUAGES

Smaller fragments of Islamic literature, in Chinese, are found in China (which has quite a large Muslim population) and in the Philippines. The literary traditions of Indonesia and of Malaysia, where the religion of Islam arrived long ago, are also worth noting. Historical and semimythical tales about Islamic heroes are a feature of the literature in these areas, a fact of immense interest to folklorists.

Contact with Islam and its "written" culture also helped to preserve national idioms in many regions. Often such idioms were enriched by Arabic vocabulary and Islamic concepts. The leaders of the Muslims in such areas in northern Nigeria, for example, preferred to write poetry and chronicles in Arabic while using their mother tongue for more popular forms of literature. Of particular interest in this connection is Kurdish literature, which has preserved in an Iranian language several important, popular heterodox texts and epics.

Chapter 2

The Forms of Islamic Literature

In order to fully understand and enjoy Eastern literature, one must study its external characteristics most carefully. The literatures of the Islamic peoples are intellectual; in neither poetry nor prose are there many examples of subjective lyricism as it is understood in the West. The principal genres, forms, and rules were inherited from pre-Islamic Arabic poetry but were substantially elaborated afterward, especially by the Persians.

Rhyme and Metre

Arabic poetry is built upon the principle of monorhyme, and the single rhyme, usually consisting in one letter, is employed throughout every poem, long or short. The structure of the Arabic language permits such monorhymes to be achieved with comparative ease. The Persians and their imitators often extended the rhyming part over two or more syllables (*radīf*) or groups of words, which are repeated after the dominant rhyming consonant. The metres are quantitative, counting long and short syllables (*ʿarūḍ*). Classical Arabic has 16 basic metres in five groupings; they can undergo certain variations, but the poet is not allowed to change the metre in the course of the poem. Syllable-counting metres, as well as strophic forms, are used in popular, or "low," poetry; only in postclassical Arabic were some strophic forms introduced into "high" poetry. Many modern Islamic poets, from Pakistan to Turkey and North Africa, have discarded the classical system of prosody altogether. In part they have substituted verse forms imitating Western models such as strophic poems with or without rhyme; since about 1950 free verse has almost become the rule, although a certain tendency toward rhyming or to the use of alliterative quasi-rhymes can be observed.

Genres

The chief poetic genres, as they emerged according to traditional rules, are the *qaṣīdah*, the *ghazal*, and the *qiṭʿah*; in Iran and its adjacent countries there are, further, the *robāʿī* and the *mas̄navī*.

Qaṣīdah

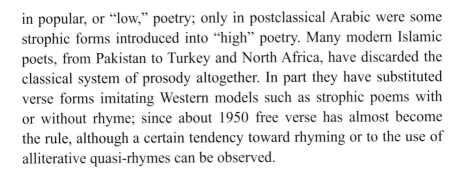

The *qaṣīdah* (literally "purpose poem"), a genre whose form was invented by pre-Islamic Arabs, has from 20 to more than 100 verses and usually contains an account of the poet's journey. In the classic pattern, the parts followed a fixed sequence, beginning with a love-poem prologue (*nasīb*), followed by a description of the journey itself, and finally reaching its real goal by flattering the poet's patron, sharply attacking some adversaries of his tribe, or else indulging in measureless self-praise. Everywhere in the Muslim world the *qaṣīdah* became the characteristic form for panegyric. It could serve for religious purposes as well: solemn praise of God, eulogies of the Prophet, and songs of praise and lament for the martyr heroes of Shīʿite Islam were all expressed in this form. Later, the introductory part of the *qaṣīdah* often was taken up by a description of nature or given over to some words of wisdom, or the poet took the opportunity to demonstrate his skill in handling extravagant language and to show off his learning. Such exhibitions were made all the more difficult because, though it varied according to the rank of the person to whom it was addressed, the vocabulary of each type of *qaṣīdah* was controlled by rigid conventions.

Ghazal

The *ghazal* possibly originated as an independent elaboration of the *qaṣīdah*'s introductory section, and it usually embodies a love poem. Ideally, its length varies between 5 and 12 verses. It can be used for either religious or secular expression, the two often being blended indistinguishably. Its diction is light and graceful, its effect comparable to that of chamber music, whereas the *qaṣīdah* writer employs, so to speak, the full orchestral resources.

Qiṭʿah

Monorhyme is used in both the *qaṣīdah* and *ghazal*. But while these two forms begin with two rhyming hemistiches (half lines of a verse), in the *qiṭʿah* ("section") the first hemistich does not rhyme, and the effect is as though the poem had been "cut out" of a longer one (hence its name). The *qiṭʿah* is a less-serious literary form that was used to deal with aspects of everyday life; it served mainly for occasional poems, satire, jokes, word games, and chronograms.

OTHER POETIC FORMS

There are a variety of other forms that are more or less restricted to folk poetry, such as the *sīḥarfī* ("golden alphabet"), in which each line or each stanza begins with succeeding letters of the Arabic alphabet. In Muslim India the *bārāīāsa* ("12 months") is a sort of lovers' calendar in which the poet, assuming the role of a young woman of longing, expresses the lover's feelings in accord with the seasons of the year. Apart from these, later writers tried to develop strophic forms. Sometimes *ghazal*s with the same metre were bound together as "stanzas" to form a longer unit through the use of a linking verse. When the linking verse was recurrent, the poem was called a *tarjīʿ-band* (literally "return-tie"); when the linking verse was varied, the poem was called a *tarkīb-band* (literally "composite-tie"). True stanzas of varying lengths were also invented. Among these, mainly in Urdu and Turkish, a six-line stanza known as *musaddas* became the form used for the *marsīyeh* (dirge for the martyrs of Karbalāʾ). Because it had come to be associated with lofty feeling and serious thought, *musaddas* later was used for the first reformist modern poems.

Robāʿī

The form of the *robāʿī*, which is a quatrain in fixed metre with a rhyme scheme of *a a b a*, seems to go back to pre-Islamic Persian poetical tradition. It has supplied the Persian poets with a flexible vehicle for ingenious aphorisms and similarly concise expressions of thought for religious, erotic, or skeptical purposes. The peoples who came under Persian cultural influence happily adopted this form.

Mas̄navī

Epic poetry was unknown to the Arabs, who were averse to fiction, whether it was expressed in poetry or in prose. The development of epic poetry was thus hindered, just as was the creation of novels or short stories. Nevertheless, *mas̄navī*—which means literally "the doubled one," or rhyming couplet, and by extension a poem consisting of a series of such couplets—became a favourite poetical form of the Persians and those cultures they influenced. The *mas̄navī* enabled the poet to develop the thread of a tale through thousands of verses. Yet even in such poetry only a restricted number of metres were employed, and no metre allowed more than 11 syllables in a hemistich. Metre and diction were prescribed in accordance with the topic; a didactic *mas̄navī* required a style and metre different from a heroic or romantic one. The *mas̄navī* usually begins with a praise of God, and this strikes the keynote of the poem.

Maqāmah

The most typical expression of the Arabic—and Islamic—spirit in prose is the *maqāmah* (meaning "gathering," "assembly"), which tells basically simple stories in an extremely and marvelously complicated style (abounding in word plays, logographs, double entendres, and the like) and which comes closest to the Western concept of the short story.

The versatility and erudition of the classical *maqāmah* authors is dazzling, but the fables and parables that, during the first centuries of Islam, had been told in a comparatively easy flowing style later became subject to a growing trend toward artificiality, as did almost every other literary genre, including expository prose. Persian historiographers and Turkish biographers, Indo-Muslim writers on mysticism, and even writers on science all indulged in a style in which rhyme and rhetoric often completely obscured the meaning. It is only since the late 19th century that a matter-of-fact style has slowly become acceptable in literary circles; the influence of translations from European languages, the role of journalism, and the growing pride in a pure language freed from the cobwebs of the past worked together to make Islamic languages more pliable and less artificial.

IMAGERY

In all forms of poetry and in most types of prose, writers shared a common fund of imagery that was gradually refined and enlarged in the course of time. The main source of imagery was the Qurʾān, its figures and utterances often divested of their sacred significance. Thus, the beautiful Joseph (sura 12) is a fitting symbol for the handsome beloved; the nightingale may sing the psalms of David (sura 21:79 and others); the rose sits on Solomon's wind-borne throne (sura 21:81 and others), and its opening petals can be compared to Joseph's shirt rent by Potiphar's wife (sura 12:25 and following), its scent to that of Joseph's shirt, which cured blind Jacob (sura 12:94). The tulip reminds the poet of the burning bush before which Moses stood (sura 20:9 and following), and the coy beloved refuses the lover's demands by answering, like God to Moses, "Thou shalt not see me" (sura 7:143); but her (or his) kiss gives the dying lover new life, like the breath of Jesus (sura 3:49).

Classical Persian poetry often mentions knights and kings from Iran's history alongside those from Arabic heroic tales. The cup of wine offered by the "old man of the Magians" is comparable to the miraculous cup owned by the Iranian mythical king Jamshīd or to Alexander's mirror, which showed the marvels of the world; the

This illustration of a garden is from a copy of the poet Jāmī's *Haft owrang*. Islamic gardens create the sense of being in a jewelled private world and are a common subject in literature.

nightingale may sing "Zoroastrian tunes" when it contemplates the "fire temple of the rose." Central scenes from the great Persian *mas̄navīs* contributed to the imagery of later writers in Persian-, Turkish-, and Urdu-speaking areas. Social and political conditions are reflected in a favourite literary equation between the "beautiful and cruel beloved" and "the Turk": because in Iran and India the military caste was usually of Turkish origin, and because the Turk was always considered handsome, in literary imagery he stood as the "ruler of hearts." Minute arabesque-like descriptions of nature, particularly of garden scenes, are frequent: the rose and the nightingale have almost become substitutes for mythological figures.

The versatile writer was expected to introduce elegant allusions to classical Arabic and Persian literature and to folklore and to know enough about astrology, alchemy, and medicine to use the relevant technical terms accurately. Images inspired by the pastimes of the grandees—chess, polo, hunting, and the like—were as necessary for a good poem as were those referring to music, painting, and calligraphy. Similarly, allusions in poetic imagery to the Arabic alphabet—often thought to be endowed with mystical significance or magical properties—were very common in all Islamic literatures.

The poet had to follow strict rules laid down by the masters of rhetoric, rigidly observing the harmonious selection of similes thought proper to any one given sphere (four allusions to Qurʾānic figures, for example, or three garden images all given in a single verse). The poet was expected to invent new fantastic etiologies (*ḥosn-e taʿlīl*): he had to describe natural phenomena in some elegant and surprising metaphor. Thus, "The narcissus has strewn silver in the way of the bride rose" means simply "The narcissus has withered"—for when the rose (dressed in red, like an Eastern bride) appears in late spring, it is time for the narcissus to shed its white petals, just as people would shed silver coins in the way of a bridal procession.

Skills Required of the Writer

The writer was also expected to use puns and to play with words of two or more meanings. He might write verses that could provide an intelligible meaning even when read backward. He had to be able to handle chronograms, codes based on the numerical values of a phrase or verse, which, when understood, gave the date of some relevant event. Later writers sometimes supplied the date of a book's compilation by hiding a chronogram in its title. A favourite device in poetry was the question-and-answer form, employed in the whole poem or only in chosen sections.

Writers were expected to demonstrate talent at both improvisation and elaboration on any theme if they wished to attract the interest of a generous patron. Poetry was judged according to the perfection of its individual verses. Only in rare cases was the poem appreciated as a whole: the lack of coherent argument, which often puzzles the Western reader in *ghazal* poetry, is in fact deliberate.

It would be idle to look for the unveiled expression of personal emotion in Arabic, Turkish, or Persian poetry. The conventions are so rigid that the reader is allowed only a rare glimpse into the poet's feelings. Indeed, such feelings were put through the sieve of intellect, and personal experiences were thereby transformed into arabesque-like work of artistry. In the hands of mediocre versifiers and prose writers, literature could become mannered and completely artificial, with the reader soon tiring of the constantly recurring moon faces, hyacinth curls, ruby lips, and cypress statures (that is, tall and slender). Yet the great masters of poetry and rhetoric (who all have their favourite imagery, rhymes, and rhythmical patterns) allow the patient reader a glimpse into their hearts by a slight rhythmical change or by a new way of expressing a conventional thought.

This illustration for the poet Ḥāfeẓ's *Dīvān* shows a reception with poetry and music. As a court poet, Ḥāfeẓ enjoyed the patronage of several rulers of Shīrāz, in what is today Iran.

These are, of course, quite crude generalizations. Folk poetry, for instance, has to be judged by different standards, though even here conventional forms and inherited imagery contribute to a certain degree of standardization. Only in the 20th century was a complete break with classical ideals made. Since then, sincerity instead of imitation, political and social commitment instead of panegyric, and realism instead of escapism have been the characteristic features of modern literatures of the Muslim countries.

CHAPTER 3

THE ROOTS OF ISLAMIC LITERATURE

The first known poetic compositions of the Arabs are of such perfect beauty and, at the same time, are so conventionalized that they raise the question as to how far back an actual poetic tradition does stretch. A great number of pre-Islamic poems, dating from the mid-6th century, were preserved by oral tradition. The seven most famous pieces are *al-Muʿallaqāt* ("The Suspended Ones," known as *The Seven Odes*), and these are discussed more fully later in this chapter. The term *muʿallaqāt* is not fully understood; later legend asserts that the seven poems had been hung in the most important Arab religious sanctuary, the Kaʿbah in Mecca, because of their eloquence and beauty and had brought victory to their authors in the poetical contests traditionally held during the season of pilgrimage. Apart from these seven, quite a number of shorter poems were preserved by later scholars. An independent genre in pre-Islamic poetry was the elegy, often composed by a woman, usually a deceased hero's sister. Some of these poems, especially those by the poet al-Khansāʾ (who died after 630) are notable for their compact expressiveness.

POETRY

The poet (called a *shāʿir*, a wizard endowed with magic powers) was thought to be inspired by a spirit (*jinn*, *shayṭān*). The poet defended the honour of his tribe and perpetuated their deeds. Religious expression was rare in pre-Islamic poetry. In the main it reflects the sense of fatalism that was probably needed if the harsh circumstances of Bedouin life in the desert were to be endured.

The most striking feature of pre-Islamic poetry is the uniformity and refinement of its language. Although the various tribes, constantly feuding with one another, all spoke their own dialects, they shared a common language for poetry whether they were Bedouins or inhabitants of the small capitals of al-Ḥīrah and Ghassān (where the influence of Aramaic culture was also in evidence).

Arabic was even then a virile and expressive language, with dozens of synonyms for the horse, the camel, the lion, and so forth; and it possessed a rich stock of descriptive adjectives. Because of those features, it is difficult for foreigners and modern Arabs alike to appreciate fully the artistic qualities of early Arabic poetry. Imagery is precise, and descriptions of natural phenomena are detailed. The sense of universal applicability is lacking, however, and the comparatively simple literary techniques of simile and metaphor predominate. The imaginative power that was later to be the hallmark of Arabic poetry under Persian influence had not yet become evident.

The strikingly rich vocabulary of classical Arabic, as well as its sophisticated structure, is matched by highly elaborate metrical schemes, based on quantity. The rhythmical structures were analyzed by the grammarian Khalīl of Basra (died *c.* 791), who distinguished 16 metres. Each was capable of variation by shortening the foot or part of it, but the basic structure was rigidly preserved. One and the same rhyme letter had to be maintained throughout the poem. (The rules of rhyming are detailed and very complicated but were followed quite strictly from the 6th to the early 20th century.)

As well as rules governing the outward form of poetry, a system of poetic imagery already existed by this early period. The

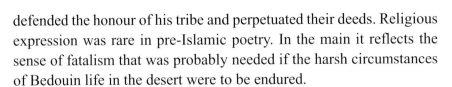

The mobility and freedom that the camel afforded to desert Arabs helped forge their independent culture. There are even *qaṣīdah* celebrating the *nāqah* (female camel) as a faithful, unwavering mount.

sequence of a poem, moreover, followed a fixed pattern (such as that for the *qaṣīdah*). Pre-Islamic poetry was not written down but recited, and sound and rhythm therefore played an important part in its formation, and the *rāwī*s (reciters) were equally vital to its preservation. A *rāwī* was associated with some famous bard and, having learned his master's techniques, might afterward become a poet himself. This kind of apprenticeship to a master whose poetic style was thus continued became a common practice in the Muslim world (especially in Muslim India) right up to the 19th century.

From pre-Islamic times the seven authors of *The Seven Odes*, already described, are usually singled out for special praise. Their poems and miscellaneous verses were collected during the 8th century and ever since have been the subject of numerous commentaries in the East. They have been studied in Europe since the early 19th century.

The poet Imruʾ al-Qays (died *c.* 550 CE), of the tribe of Kindah, was foremost both in time and in poetic merit. He was a master of love poetry; his frank descriptions of dalliance with his mistresses are considered so seductive that (as orthodox Puritanism claims) the Prophet Muhammad called him "the leader of poets on the way to Hell." His style is supple and picturesque. It grips the attention whether his poems sing of his love adventures or describe a seemingly endless rainy night. Of all classical Arabic poets he is probably the one who appeals most to modern taste. At the other extreme stands Zuhayr, praising the chiefs of the rival tribes of ʿAbs and Dhubyān for ending a long feud. He is chiefly remembered for his serious *qaṣīdah* in which, old, wise, and experienced, he meditates upon the terrible escalation

The Romance of ʿAntar evolved out of a Bedouin tradition that stressed nobility of character and desert chivalry and of which ʿAntar was the epitome. This Syrian illustration shows ʿAntar on horseback.

THE OUTLAW POETS

Exciting for their savagery and beauty are poems by Taʾabbaṭa Sharran and al-Shanfarā, both outlaw warriors. Their verses reveal the wildness of Bedouin life, with its ideals of bravery, revenge, and hospitality. Taʾabbaṭa Sharran is the author of the widely translated *Song of Revenge* (for his uncle), composed in a short, sharp metre. Shanfarā's *lāmiyyah* (literally "poem rhyming in [the letter] l") vividly, succinctly, and with a wealth of detail tells of the experiences to be had from life in the desert. This latter poem has sometimes been considered a forgery, created by a learned grammarian. The suggestion highlights the question, often posed, of how much pre-Islamic poetry is genuine and how much is the product of later scholars. Some modern critics—without proper justification—would dismiss the entire corpus as counterfeit.

of war. Various aspects of Bedouin life, as well as the attitude of the Arabs to the rulers of the small kingdom of Al-Ḥīrah on the Euphrates River, are reflected in the poems of al-Nābighah al-Dhubyānī, ʿAmr ibn Kulthūm, and Ṭarafah ibn al-ʿAbd. The boastful pride of the self-centred Arab warrior can be observed best in the poems of al-Ḥārith, who became proverbial for his arrogance. ʿAntarah ibn Shaddād, son of an Arab king and a black slave girl, won such fame on the battlefield and for his poetry that he later became the hero of the *Romance of ʿAntar*, an Arabic folk romance.

PROSE

While poetry forms the most important part of early Arabic literature and is an effective historical preservation of the Arab past glory, there is also a quantity of prose. Of special interest is the rhymed prose (*saj*ʿ) peculiar to soothsayers, which developed into an important form of ornate prose writing in every Islamic country. Tales about the adventures and battle days of the various tribes (*ayyām al-ʿArab*, or "The Days of the Arabs") were told and handed down from generation to generation, usually interspersed with pieces of poetry. Proverbs and proverbial sayings were as common as in most cultures at a comparable level of development. The "literary" genre most typical of Bedouin life is the *musāmarah*, or "nighttime conversation," in which the central subject is elaborated not by plot but by verbal associations that direct the listener's mind from topic to topic. Thus, the language as language played a most important role. The *musāmarah* form inspired the later *maqāmah* literature.

It has been said—and this certainly holds true for the *musāmarah*—that Arabic literature demands attention from its listeners only in short bursts, for listeners are carried from verse to verse, from anecdote to anecdote, from pun to pun, along a theme whose broad outline is entirely familiar. Western scholars of the East have for this reason spoken of the "molecular," or "atomic," structure both of classical Arabic literature and of traditional Islamic thought. An audience listening to one of the ancient bards—or to a modern poet or orator in the Muslim world—would be able to listen without tiring. The sheer emotive power of the Arabic language to enrapture and bewitch its listeners by sound alone should be kept in mind when any piece of Arabic literature is considered. Only a people endowed with peculiar sensibility to the word could properly appreciate the refinement of pre-Islamic poetry and be ready to accept the concept of divine revelation appearing through the word in the Qurʾān.

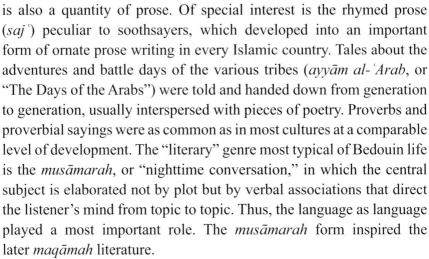

Chapter 4

Early Islamic Literature

With the coming of Islam, the attitude of the Arabs toward poetry seems to have changed. The new Muslims, despite their long-standing admiration for powerful language, often shunned poetry as reminiscent of pagan ideals now overthrown, for the Qurʾān (in sura 26:225 and following) condemned the poets "who err in every valley, and say what they do not do. Only the perverse follow them!" The Qurʾān, as the revealed word of God, was now considered the supreme manifestation of literary beauty. It became the basis and touchstone of almost every cultural and literary activity and attained a unique position in Arabic literature.

Age of the Caliphs

It might be expected that a new and vigorous religion would stimulate a new religious literature to sing of its greatness and glory. This, however, was not the case. Maybe the once-boastful poets felt, at least for a while, that they were nothing but humble servants of Allah. At any rate, no major poet was inspired by the birth and astonishingly rapid expansion of Islam. Only much later did poets claim that their work was the "heritage of prophecy" or draw upon a tradition that calls the tongues of the poets "the keys of the treasures beneath the Divine Throne." The old, traditional literary models were still faithfully followed: a famous ode by Kaʿb, the son of Zuhayr, is different from pre-Islamic poetry only insofar as it ends in praise of the Prophet, imploring his forgiveness, instead of eulogizing some Bedouin leader. Muhammad's eulogist, Ḥassān ibn Thābit (died *c.* 659), also repeated the traditional patterns (even including the praise of wine that had been such a common feature of pre-Islamic poetry at the court of al-Ḥīrah, despite the fact that wine had been by then religiously prohibited).

Religious themes are to be found in the *khuṭbah*s, or Friday sermons, which were delivered by governors of the provinces. In these *khuṭbah*s, however, political considerations frequently overshadowed the religious and literary aspects. The *quṣṣās* (storytellers), who interpreted verses from the Qurʾān, attracted large

This 13th-century miniature is by the Iraqi painter and illustrator Yaḥyā ibn Maḥmūd al-Wāsiṭī. It shows a crowd listening to a *khuṭbah* being delivered from the *minbar* of a mosque.

audiences and may be regarded as the inventors of a popular religious prose. Their interpretations were highly fanciful, however, and hardly squared with the theologian's orthodoxy.

The desire to preserve words of wisdom is best reflected in the sayings attributed to ʿAlī, the fourth caliph (died 661). These, however, were written down, in superbly concise diction, only in the 10th century under the title *Nahj al-balāghah* ("The Path of Eloquence"), a work that is a masterpiece of the finest Arabic prose and that has inspired numerous commentaries and poetical variations in the various languages of the Islamic world.

Umayyad Dynasty

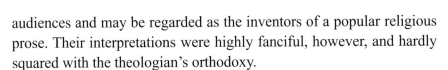

The time of the "Four Righteous Caliphs," as it is called, ended with ʿAlī's assassination in 661. The Umayyad dynasty then gained the throne, and a new impetus in poetry soon became perceptible. The Umayyads were by no means a pious dynasty, much enjoying the pleasures of life in their residence in Damascus and in their luxurious castles in the Syrian desert. One of their last rulers, the profligate al-Walīd ibn Yazīd (died 744), has become famous not so much as a conqueror (although in 711 the Muslims reached the lower Indus basin, Transoxania, and Spain) but as a poet who excelled in frivolous love verses and poetry in praise of wine. He was fond of short, light metres to match his subjects and rejected the heavier metres preferred by *qaṣīdah* writers. His verses convey a sense of ease and gracious living. Al-Walīd was not, however, the first to attempt this kind of poetry: a remarkable poet from Mecca, ʿUmar ibn Abī Rabīʿah (died *c.* 712/719), had contributed in large measure to the separate development of the love poem (*ghazal*) from its subordinate place as the opening section of the *qaṣīdah*. Gentle and charming, written in attractive and lively rhythms, his poems sing of amorous adventures with the ladies who came to Mecca on pilgrimage. His lighthearted melodious poems still appeal to modern readers.

In Medina, on the other hand, idealized love poetry was the vogue; its invention is attributed to Jamīl (died 701), of the tribe ʿUdhrah, "whose members die when they love." The names of some of these "martyrs of love," together with the names of their beloveds, were preserved and eventually became proverbial expressions of the tremendous force of true love. Such was Imruʾ al-Qays, who went mad because of his passion for Laylā and was afterward known as Majnūn (the "Demented One"). His story is cherished by later Persian, Turkish, and Urdu poets; as a symbol of complete surrender to the force of love, he is dear both to religious mystics and to secular poets.

Despite such new developments, the traditional *qaṣīdah* form of poetry was by no means neglected during the Umayyad period. Moreover, as the satirists of Iraq rose to fame, the *naqāʾiḍ* (slanging matches on parallel themes) between Jarīr (died *c.* 729) and al-Farazdaq (died *c.* 728 or 730) excited and delighted tribesmen of the rival settlements of Basra and Kūfah (places that later also became rival centres of philological and theological schools). The work of these two poets has furnished critics and historians with rich material for a study of the political and social situation in the early 9th century. The wealth of al-Farazdaq's vocabulary led one of the old Arabic critics to declare: "If Farazdaq's poetry did not exist, one-third of the Arabic language would be lost." Philologists, eager to preserve as much of the classical linguistic heritage as possible, have also paid a great deal of attention to the largely satirical poetry of al-Ḥuṭayʾah (died 674). The fact that Christians as well as Muslims were involved in composing classical Arabic poetry is proved by the case of al-Akhṭal (died *c.* 710), whose work preserves the pre-Islamic tradition of al-Ḥīrah in authentic form. He is particularly noted for his wine songs. Christians and Jews had been included among the pre-Islamic poets.

Hadith record the traditions or sayings of the Prophet Muhammad, revered as a major source of religious law and moral guidance. These pages are from a copy of the Hadith collected by Muslim ibn al-Ḥajjāj.

Prose literature was still restricted to religious writing. The traditions of the Prophet (Hadith) began to be compiled, and, after careful sifting, those regarded as trustworthy were preserved in six great collections during the late 9th century. Two of these—that of al-Bukhārī and that of Muslim ibn al-Ḥajjāj—were considered second only to the Qurʾān in religious importance. The first studies of religious law and legal problems, closely connected with the study of the Qurʾān, also belong to that period.

The ʿAbbāsids

It was not until the ʿAbbāsids assumed power in 750, settling in Baghdad, that the golden age of Arabic literature began. The influx of foreign elements added new colour to cultural and literary life.

Hellenistic thought and the influence of the ancient cultures of the Middle East, for example, contributed to the rapid intellectual growth of the Muslim community. Its members, seized with insatiable intellectual curiosity, began to adapt elements from all the earlier high cultures and to incorporate them into their own. They thus created the wonderful fabric of Islamic culture that was so much admired in the Middle Ages by western Europe. Indian and Iranian threads were also woven into this fabric, and a new sensitivity to beauty in the field of poetry and the fine arts was cultivated.

The classical Bedouin style was still predominant in literature and was the major preoccupation of grammarians. These men were, as the modern critic Sir Hamilton Gibb emphasized, the true humanists of Islam. Their efforts helped to standardize "High Arabic," giving it an unchangeable structure once and for all. By then the inhabitants of the growing towns in Iraq and Syria were beginning to express their love, hatred, religious fervour, and frivolity in a style more appealing to their fellow townsmen. Poets no longer belonged exclusively to what had been the Bedouin aristocracy. Artisans and freed slaves, of non-Arab origin, were included among their number. Bashshār ibn Burd (died *c.* 784), the son of a Persian slave, was the first representative of the new style. This ugly, blind workman excelled as a seductive love poet and also as a biting satirist—"Nobody could be secure from the itch of his tongue," it was later said—and he added a new degree of expressiveness to the old forms. The category of *zuhdiyyah* (ascetic poems) was invented by the poet Abū al-ʿAtāhiyyah (died 825/826) from Basra, the centre of early ascetic movements. His pessimistic thoughts on the transitory nature of this world were uttered in an unpretentious kind of verse that rejected all current notions of style and technical finesse. He had turned to ascetic poetry after efforts at composing love songs.

The same is said of Abū Nuwās (died *c.* 813/815), the most outstanding of the ʿAbbāsid poets. His witty and cynical verses are addressed mainly to handsome boys; best known are his scintillating drinking songs. His line "Accumulate as many sins as you can" seems to have been his motto, and, compared with some of his more lascivious lines, even the most daring passages of pre-Islamic poetry sound chaste. Abū Nuwās had such an incomparable command over the language, however, that he came to be regarded as one of the greatest Arabic poets of all time. Nevertheless, orthodox Muslims would quote of him and of his imitators the Prophet's alleged saying that "poetry is what Satan has spit out," since he not only described subjects prohibited by religious law but praised them with carefree lightheartedness.

This statue of Abū Nuwās is in Baghdad. The language of the poet's *qaṣīdahs* is grammatically sound and based on the old Arab traditions. His themes, however, are drawn from urban life, not the desert.

The "New" Style

The new approach to poetry that developed during the 9th century was first accorded scholarly discussion in the *Kitāb al-badīʿ* (*The Book of Tropes*) by Ibn al-Muʿtazz (died 908), caliph for one day, who laid down rules for the use of metaphors, similes, and verbal puns. The ideal of these "modern" poets was the richest possible embellishment of verses by the use of tropes, brilliant figures of speech, and far-fetched poetic conceits. Many later handbooks of poetics discussed these rules in minute detail, and eventually the increasing use of rhetorical devices produced artificiality. (Ibn al-Muʿtazz was himself a fine poet whose descriptions of courtly life and nature are lovely; he even tried to compose an epic poem, a genre otherwise unknown to the Arabs.) The "modern" poets, sensitive to colours, sounds, and shapes, were also fond of writing short poems on unlikely subjects: a well-bred hunting dog or an inkpot; delicious sweetmeats or jaundice; the ascetic who constantly weeps when he remembers his sins; the luxurious garden parties of the rich; an elegy for a cat; or a description of a green ewer. Their amusing approach, however, was sooner or later bound to lead to mannered compositions. The growing use of colour images may be credited to the increasing Persian influence upon ʿAbbāsid poetry, for the Persian poets were, as has been often observed, on the whole more disposed to visual than to acoustic imagery.

New attitudes toward love, too, were being gradually developed in poetry. Eventually, what was to become a classic theme, that of *ḥubb ʿudhrī* ("ʿUdhrah love")—the lover would rather die than achieve union with his beloved—was expounded by the Ẓāhirī theologian Ibn Dāʾūd (died 910) in his poetic anthology *Kitāb al-zahrah* (*The Book of the Flower*). This theme was central to the *ghazal* poetry of the following centuries. Although at first completely secular, it was later taken over as a major concept in mystical love poetry. (The first examples of this adoption, in Iraq and Egypt, took place in Ibn Dāʾūd's lifetime.) The wish to die on the path that leads to the beloved became commonplace in Persian, Turkish, and Urdu poetry, and most romances in these languages end tragically. Ibn Dāʾūd's influence also spread to the western Islamic world. A century after his death, the theologian Ibn Ḥazm (died 1064), drawing upon personal experiences, composed in Spain his famous work on "pure love" called *Ṭawq al-ḥamāmah* (*The Ring of the Dove*). Its lucid prose, interspersed with poetry, has many times been translated into Western languages.

The conflict between the traditional ideals of poetry and the "modern" school of the early ʿAbbāsid period also led to the growth of a literary criticism, the criteria of which were largely derived from the study of Greek philosophy.

Traditional poetry, meanwhile, was not neglected, but its style was somewhat modified in accordance with the new ideas. Two famous anthologies of Bedouin poetry, both called *Ḥamāsah* ("Poems of Bravery"), were collected by the Syrian Abū Tammām (died *c.* 845) and his disciple al-Buḥturī (died 897), both noted classical poets in their own right. They provide an excellent survey of those poems from the stock of early Arabic poetry that were considered worth preserving. A century later Abū al-Faraj al-Iṣbahānī (died 967), in a multivolume work entitled *Kitāb al-aghānī* ("Books of Songs"), collected a great number of poems and biographical notes on poets and musicians. This material gives a colourful and valuable panorama of literary life in the first four centuries of Islam.

In the mid-10th century a new cultural centre emerged at the small court of the Ḥamdānids in Aleppo. Here the Central Asian scholar al-Fārābī (died 950) wrote his fundamental works on philosophy and musical theory. Here too, for a while, lived Abū al-Ṭayyib al-Mutanabbī (died 965), who is in the mainstream of

Ibn Ḥazm was famed for his literary productivity, breadth of learning, and mastery of the Arabic language. This statue of him stands in his birthplace, Córdoba, Spain.

classical *qaṣīdah* writers but who surpasses them all in the extravagance of what has been called his "reckless audacity of imagination." He combined some elements of Iraqi and Syrian stylistics with classical ingredients. His compositions—panegyrics of rulers and succinct verses (which are still quoted)—have never ceased to intoxicate the Arabs by their daring hyperbole, their marvelous sound effects, and their formal perfection. Western readers are unlikely to derive as much aesthetic pleasure from Mutanabbī's poetry as do speakers of Arabic. They will probably prefer the delicate verses about gardens and flowers by Mutanabbī's colleague in Aleppo, al-Ṣanawbarī (died 945), a classic exponent of the descriptive style. This style in time reached Spain, where the superb garden and landscape poetry of Ibn Khafājah (died 1139) displayed an even higher degree of elegance and sensitivity than that of his Eastern predecessors.

Before turning to the development of prose, it is necessary to mention a figure unique among those writing in Arabic. This was al-Maʿarrī (died 1057), a blind poet of Syria, the sincerity and humanity of whose verses continue to appeal greatly to young Arabs. But al-Maʿarrī's vocabulary is so difficult, his verses, with their double rhymes, are so compressed in meaning, that even his contemporaries, flocking to his lectures, had to ask him to interpret their significance. His outlook is deeply pessimistic and skeptical. Although his poems display a mastery of the Arabic traditional stylistic devices, they run counter to the conventional ideals of Arab heroism by speaking of bitter disappointment and emphasizing asceticism, compassion, and the avoidance of procreation.

> Taking reason for his guide he judges men and things with a freedom which must have seemed scandalous to the rulers and privileged classes of the day. Among his meditations on the human tragedy a fierce hatred of injustice, hypocrisy, and

> superstition blazes out. Vice and folly are laid bare in order that virtue and wisdom may be sought…

says Reynold A. Nicholson, al-Maʿarrī's foremost interpreter in the West, who also translated his *Risālat al-ghufrān* ("The Epistle of Forgiveness"; Eng. trans. *Risalat ul Ghufran: A Divine Comedy*), which describes a visit to the otherworld. Maʿarrī's extremely erudite book also contains sarcastic criticism of Arabic literature. His *Al-Fuṣūl wa al-ghāyāt* ("Paragraphs and Periods") is an ironic commentary on humanity and nature but is presented as a sequence of pious exhortations in rhymed prose. It has scandalized the pious, some of whom see it as a parody of the Qurʾān. Maʿarrī's true intention in writing this book is unknown.

DEVELOPMENT OF LITERARY PROSE

During the ʿAbbāsid period, literary prose also began to develop. Ibn al-Muqaffaʿ (died *c.* 756), of Persian origin, translated the fables of Bidpai into Arabic under the title *Kalīlah wa Dimnah*. These fables provided Islamic culture with a seemingly inexhaustible treasure of tales and parables, which are to be found in different guises throughout the whole of Muslim literature. He also introduced into Arabic the fictitious chronicles of the Persian *Khvatāy-nāmak* ("Book of Kings"). This was the source of a kind of pre-Islamic mythology that the literati preferred above the somewhat meagre historical accounts of the Arab pagan past otherwise available to them. These activities demanded a smooth prose style, and Ibn al-Muqaffaʿ has therefore rightly been regarded as the inaugurator of what is called "secretarial literature" (that produced by secretaries in the official chancelleries). He also translated writings on ethics and the conduct of government, which helped to determine the rules of etiquette (*adab*). His works are the prototype of the "Mirror for Princes" literature, which flourished during the late Middle Ages both in Iran and in the West. In this literature a legendary Persian counselor, Bozorgmehr, was presented as a paragon of wise conduct. Later, stories were invented that combined Qur᾿ānic heroes with historical characters from the Iranian past.

A growing interest in things outside the limits of Bedouin life was reflected in a quantity of didactic yet entertaining prose by such masters as the broad-minded and immensely learned al-Jāḥiẓ (died 869). In response to the wide-ranging curiosity of urban society, the list of his subjects includes treatises on theology, on misers, on donkeys, and on thieves. His masterpiece is *Kitāb al-ḥayawān* ("The Book of Animals"), which has little to do with zoology but is a mine

Al-Jāḥiẓ's *Kitāb al-ḥayawān* is a bestiary drawing on Aristotle and also an anthology of Arabic literature with animal themes to which theological, sociological, and linguistic discussions have been added.

of information about Arab proverbs, traditions, superstitions, and the like. Al-Jāḥiẓ's style is vigorous, loquacious, and uninhibited. His work, however, is not well constructed, and it lacks the clear sobriety of the "secretarial style." Yet the glimpses it affords into the life of various strata of society during the 9th century have rightly attracted the special interest of Western scholars. Less impressive, but almost as multifaceted, are the treatises of Ibn Abī al-Dunyā (died 894).

The concept of *adab* was soon enlarged to include not only educational prose dealing with etiquette for all classes of people but belles lettres in general. The classic example of Arabic style for prose writers in this field, accepted as such for almost a millennium, is the writing of the Persian Ibn Qutaybah (died 889). His *Kitab ʿuyūn al-akhbār* ("Book of Choice Narratives"), in 10 books, each dealing with a given subject, provided a model to which numberless essayists in the Muslim world conformed. In his book on poetry and poets, Ibn Qutaybah dared, for the first time, to doubt openly that pre-Islamic poetry was incomparable. The most vigorous prose style was achieved by Abū Ḥayyān al-Tawḥīdī (died 1023), who portrayed the weaknesses of the two leading viziers, both notorious for their literary ambitions, "...with such bitterness," as Gibb remarks, "that the book was reputed to bring misfortune upon all who possessed a copy." This work, like others by Tawḥīdī that have quite recently been discovered, reveals the author's sagacity and striking eloquence. His correspondence on problems of philosophy with Ibn Miskawayh (died 1030), the author of a widely circulated book on ethics and of a general history, helps to complete the picture of this extraordinary writer.

Sometime about 800 the Arabs had learned the art of papermaking from the Chinese. Thenceforth, cheap writing material was available, and literary output was prodigious. The *Fihrist* ("Index"), compiled by the bookseller Ibn al-Nadīm in 988, gave a full account of the Arabic literature extant in the 10th century.

It covered all kinds of literature, from philology to alchemy, but most of these works unfortunately have been lost. In those years manuals of composition (*inshā'*) were written elaborating the technique of secretarial correspondence, and they grew into an accepted genre in Arabic as well as in Persian and Turkish literature. The devices thought indispensable for elegance in modern poetry were applied to prose. The products were mannered, full of puns, verbal tricks, riddles, and the like. The new style, which was also to affect the historian's art in later times, makes a good deal of this post-classical Arabic prose look very different from the terse and direct expression characteristic of the early specimens. Rhymed prose, which at one time had been reserved for such religious occasions as the Friday sermons, was now regarded as an essential part of elegant style.

This rhetorical artistry found its most superb expression in the *maqāmah*, a form invented by al-Hamadhānī (died 1008). Its master, however, was al-Ḥarīrī (died 1122), postmaster (head of the intelligence service) at Basra and an accomplished writer on grammatical subjects. His 50 *maqāmah*s, which tell the adventures of Abū Zayd al-Sarūjī, with a wealth of language and learning, come closer to the Western concept of short story than anything else in classical Arabic literature. They abound in verbal conceits, ambivalence, assonance, alliteration, palindromes; they change abruptly from earnest to jest, from the crude to the most sublime, as the mid-20th-century scholar G.E. von Grunebaum pointed out in his evaluation of this form, which he regarded as the most typical literary reflection of the Islamic spirit. The work of al-Ḥarīrī has certainly been widely admired in the East; it has been imitated in Syriac and in Hebrew and has formed part of the syllabus in Muslim high schools of India. The pleasure to be derived from the brilliant artifice and ingenuity behind such compositions has led to their being imitated in other literary fields: quite often, in later Persian literature, one finds poems—sometimes whole books—composed of letters without diacritical marks (which distinguish otherwise similar-looking letters) or even made up entirely of unconnected letters. In India, even a commentary on the Qurʾān, in undotted letters, was written (by Fayzī, died 1595).

Achievements in the Western Muslim World

The Arabic literature of Moorish Spain and of the whole Maghrib developed parallel with that of the eastern countries but came to full flower somewhat later. Córdoba, the seat of the Umayyad rulers, was the centre of cultural life. Its wonderful mosque inspired Muslim poets right up to the 20th century (such as Sir Muḥammad Iqbāl, whose Urdu ode, *The Mosque of Córdoba*, was written in 1935). Moorish Spain was a favourite topic for reformist novelists of 19th-century Muslim India, who contrasted their own country's troubled state with the glory of classical Islamic civilization. Moorish Spain reached its cultural, political, and literary heyday under ʿAbd al-Raḥmān III (ruled 912–961). Literary stylistic changes, as noted in Iraq and Syria, spread to the west: there the old Bedouin style had always been rare and soon gave way to descriptive poetry and love poetry. Ibn Hāniʾ (died 973) of Sevilla (Seville) has been praised as the western counterpart of al-Mutanabbī, largely because of his eulogies of the Fāṭimid caliph al-Muʿizz, who at that time still resided in North Africa. The entertaining prose style of Ibn ʿAbd Rabbih (died 940) in his *Al-ʿIqd al-farīd* ("The Unique Necklace") is similar to that of his elder contemporary Ibn Qutaybah, and his book in fact became more famous than that of his predecessor. Writers on music and philology also flourished in Spain; literary criticism was practiced by Ibn Rashīq (died 1064) and, later, by al-Qarṭājannī (died 1285) in Tunis. Ibn Ḥazm (died 1064), theologian and accomplished writer on pure love, has already been mentioned.

Philosophy: Averroës and Avicenna

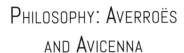

Avicenna's *Kitāb al-shifāʾ* (*Book of the Cure*) is a vast philosophical and scientific encyclopaedia. His *Al-Qānūn fī al-ṭibb* (*The Canon of Medicine*) is among the most famous books in the history of medicine.

Philosophy, medicine, and theology, all of which flourished in the ʿAbbāsid East, were also of importance in the Maghrib, and from there strong influences reached medieval Europe. The influences often came through the mediation of the Jews, who, along with numerous Christians, were largely Arabized in their cultural and literary outlook. The eastern Muslim countries could boast of the first systematic writers in the field of philosophy, including al-Kindī (died *c.* 870), al-Fārābī (died 950), and especially Avicenna (Ibn Sīnā, died 1037). Avicenna's work in philosophy, science, and medicine was outstanding and was appreciated as such in Europe. He also composed religious treatises and tales with a mystical slant. One of his romances was reworked by the Maghribi philosopher Ibn Ṭufayl (died 1185/86) in his book *Ḥayy ibn Yaqẓān* ("Alive Son of Awake"; Eng. trans. *Ibn Tufayl's Hayy ibn Yaqzan: A Philosophical Tale*, 2009). It is the story of a self-taught man who lived on a lonely island and who, in his maturity, attained the full knowledge taught by philosophers and prophets. This theme was elaborated often in later European literature.

The dominating figure in the kingdom of the Almohads, however, was the philosopher Averroës (Ibn Rushd, died 1198), court physician of the Amazigh (Berber) kings in Marrākush (Marrakech) and famous as the great Arab commentator on Aristotle. The importance of his frequently misinterpreted philosophy in the formation of medieval Christian thought is well known. Among his many other writings, especially notable is his merciless reply to an attack on philosophy made by al-Ghazālī (died 1111). Al-Ghazālī had called his attack *Tahāfut al-falāsifah* (*The Incoherence of the Philosophers*), while Averroës's equally famous reply was entitled *Tahāfut tahāfut* (*The Incoherence of the Incoherence*).

The Persian-born al-Ghazālī had, after giving up a splendid scholarly career, become the most influential representative of moderate Sufism. His chief work, *Iḥyāʾ ʿulūm al-dīn* ("The Revival of the Religious Sciences"), was based on personal religious experiences and is a perfect introduction to the pious Muslim's way to God. It inspired much later religious poetry and prose.

The numerous writings by mystics, who often expressed their wisdom in rather cryptic language (thereby contributing to the profundity of Arabic vocabulary), and the handbooks of religious teaching produced in eastern Arab and Persian areas (Sarrāj, Kalābādhī, Qushayrī, and, in Muslim India, al-Hujwīrī) are generally superior to those produced in western Muslim countries. Yet the greatest Islamic theosophist of all, Ibn al-ʿArabī (died 1240), was Spanish in origin and was educated in the Spanish tradition. His writings, in both poetry and prose, shaped large parts of Islamic thought during the following centuries. Much of the later literature of eastern Islam, particularly Persian and Indo-Persian mystical writings, indeed, can be understood only in the light of his teachings. Ibn al-ʿArabī's lyrics are typical *ghazal*s, sweet and flowing. From the late 9th century, Arabic-speaking mystics had been composing verses often meant to be sung in their meetings. At first a purely religious vocabulary was employed, but soon the expressions began to oscillate between worldly and heavenly love. The ambiguity thus achieved eventually became a characteristic feature of Persian and Turkish lyrics. Among the Arabs, religious poetry mainly followed the classical *qaṣīdah* models, and the poets lavishly decorated their panegyrics to the Prophet Muhammad with every conceivable rhetorical embellishment. Examples of this trend include *Al-Burdah* (Eng. trans. *The Poem of the Scarf* and *The Prophet's Mantle*) of al-Buṣīrī (died 1298), upon which dozens of commentaries have been written (and which has been translated into most of the languages spoken by Muslims because of the power to bless attributed to it). More sophisticated but less well known is an ode on the Prophet by the Iraqi poet Ṣafī al-Dīn al-Ḥilli (died 1350), which contains 151 rhetorical figures. The "letters of spiritual guidance" developed by the mystics are worth mentioning as a literary genre. They have been popular everywhere; from the western Islamic world the letters of Ibn ʿAbbād (died 1390) of Ronda (in Spain) are outstanding examples of this category, being written clearly and lucidly.

Geographical Literature

The Maghrib also made a substantial contribution to geographical literature, a field eagerly cultivated by Arab scholars since the 9th century. The Sicilian geographer al-Sharīf al-Idrīsī produced a famous map of the world and accompanied it with a detailed description in his *Kitāb nuzhat al-mushtāq fī ikhtirāq al-āfāq* (1154; "The Pleasure Excursion of One Who Is Eager to Traverse the Regions of the World"), which he dedicated to his patron, Roger II. The Spanish traveler Ibn Jubayr (died 1217), while on pilgrimage to Mecca, kept notes of his experiences and adventures. The resulting book became a model for the later pilgrims' manuals that are found everywhere in the Muslim world. The Maghribi explorer Ibn Baṭṭūṭah (died 1368/69 or 1377) described his extensive travels to East Asia, India, and Mali in a book filled with information about the cultural state of the Muslim world at that time. The value of his narrative is enhanced by the simple and pleasing style in which it was written.

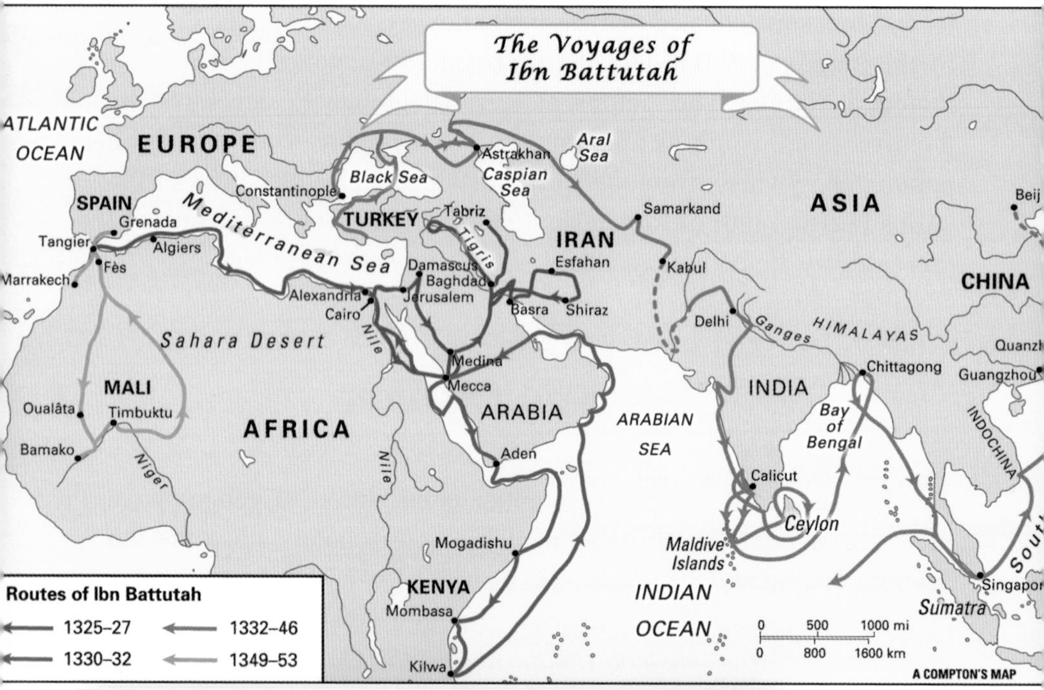

This map traces the voyages of Ibn Baṭṭūṭah. A curious observer interested in the ways of life in various countries, Ibn Baṭṭūṭah described his experiences with a human approach rarely encountered in official historiography.

IBN KHALDŪN

Any survey of western Muslim literary achievements would be incomplete if it did not mention the most profound historiographer of the Islamic world, the Tunisian Ibn Khaldūn (died 1406). History has been called the characteristic science of the Muslims because of the Qur᾿ānic admonition to discover signs of the divine in the fate of past peoples. Islamic historiography has produced histories of the Muslim conquests, world histories, histories of dynasties, court annals, and biographical works classified by occupation—scholars, poets, and theologians. Yet, notwithstanding their learning, none of the earlier writers had attempted to produce a comprehensive view of history. Ibn Khaldūn, in the famous *Muqaddimah* ("Introduction") to a projected general history, *Kitāb al-ʿibar*, sought to explain the basic factors in the historical development of the Islamic countries. His own experiences, gained on a variety of political missions in North Africa, proved useful in establishing general principles that he could apply to the manifestations of Islamic civilization. He created, in fact, the first "sociological" study of history, free from bias. Yet his book was little appreciated by his fellow historians, who still clung to the method of accumulating facts without shaping them into a well-structured whole. Ibn Khaldūn's work eventually attracted the interest of Western scholars of Asia, historians, and sociologists alike, and some of his analyses are still held in great esteem.

POETRY

In the field of poetry, Spain, which produced a considerable number of masters in the established poetical forms, also began to popularize strophic poetry, possibly deriving from indigenous models. The *muwashshaḥ* ("girdled") poem, written in the classical short metres and arranged in four- to six-line stanzas, was elaborated, enriched by internal rhymes, and, embodying some popular expressions in the poem's final section, soon achieved a standardized form. The theme is almost always love. Among the greatest lyric poets of Spain was Ibn Zaydūn of Córdoba (died 1071), who was of noble birth. After composing some charming love songs dedicated to the Umayyad princess Wallādah, he turned his hand to poetic epistles. He is the author of a beautiful *muwashshaḥ* about his hometown, which many later poets imitated. When the *muwashshaḥ* was transplanted to the eastern Arabic countries, however, it lost its original spontaneity. Another strophic form developed in Spain is the songlike *zajal* (melody), interesting for its embodiment of dialect phrases and the use of occasional words from Romance languages. Its master was Ibn Quzmān of Córdoba (died 1160), whose lifestyle was similar to that of Western troubadours. His approach to life as expressed in these melodious poems, together with their mixed idiom, suggests an interrelationship with the vernacular troubadour poetry of Spain and France.

Chapter 5

Middle Period: The Rise of Persian and Turkish Poetry

After the fall of Baghdad in 1258, Cairo became the centre of Muslim learning. Historians there recorded every detail of the daily life and the policies of the Mamlūk sultans; theologians and philologists worked under the patronage of Turkish and Circassian rulers who often did not speak a word of Arabic. The amusing semicolloquial style of the historian Ibn Iyās (died after 1521) is an interesting example of the deterioration of the Arabic language. While classical Arabic was still the ideal of the literate, it had become exclusively a "learned" language. Even some copyists who transcribed classical works showed a deplorable lack of grammatical knowledge. The literary masterpieces of this period are not works in Arabic but poetry written in Persian and Turkish.

The New Persian Style

During the ʿAbbāsid period the Persian influence upon Arabic literature had grown considerably. At the same time, a distinct Modern Persian literature came into existence in northeastern Iran, where the house of the Sāmānids of Bukhara and Samarkand had revived the memory of Sāsānian glories. The first famous representative of this new literature was the poet Rūdakī (died 940/941), of whose *qaṣīdah*s only a few have survived. He also worked on a Persian version of *Kalīlah wa Dimnah*, however, and on a version of the *Sendbād-nāmeh* ("The Book of Sendbād [Sindbad]"). Rūdakī's poetry, modeled on the Arabic rules of prosody that without exception had been applied to Persian, already points ahead to many of the characteristic features of later Persian poetry. The imagery in particular is sophisticated, although when compared with the mannered writing of subsequent times his verse was considered sadly simple. From the 10th century onward Persian poems were written at almost every court in the Iranian areas, sometimes in dialectical variants (for example, in Ṭabarestāni dialect at the Zeyārid court). In many cases the poets were bilingual, excelling in both Arabic and Persian (a gift shared by many non-Arab writers up to the 19th century).

The first significant Persian poet was Rūdakī. He flourished in the 10th century, when the Sāmānids were at the height of their power. This statue of him stands in Dushanbe, Tajikistan.

INFLUENCE OF MAḤMŪD OF GHAZNA

The first important centre of Persian literature existed at Ghazna (present-day Ghaznī, Afghanistan), at the court of Maḥmūd of Ghazna (died 1030) and his successors, who eventually extended their empire to northwestern India. Himself an orthodox warrior, Maḥmūd in later love poetry was transformed into a symbol of "a slave of his slave" because of his love for a Turkmen officer, Ayāz. Under the Ghaznavids, lyric and epic poetry both developed, as did the panegyric. Classical Iranian topics became the themes of poetry, resulting in such diverse works as the love story of Vāmeq and ʿAzrā (possibly of Greek origin) and the *Shāh-nāmeh*. A number of gifted poets praised Maḥmūd, his successors, and his ministers. Among them was Farrokhī of Seistan (died 1037), who wrote a powerful elegy on Maḥmūd's death, one of the finest compositions of Persian court poetry.

Epic and Romance

The main literary achievement of the Ghaznavid period, however, was that of Ferdowsī (died *c.* 1020). He compiled the inherited tales and legends about the Persian kings in one grand epic, the *Shāh-nāmeh* ("Book of Kings"), which contains between 35,000 and 60,000 verses in short rhyming couplets. It deals with the history of Iran from its beginnings—that is, from the "time" of the mythical kings—passing on to historical events, giving information about the acceptance of the Zoroastrian faith, Alexander's invasion, and, eventually, the conquest of the country by the Arabs. A large part of the work centres on tales of the hero Rostam. These stories are essentially

This page from a 15th-century copy of the *Shāh-nāmeh* shows the hero Esfandīār attacking a mythical bird called the Sīmurgh.

part of a different culture, thus revealing something about the Indo-European sources of Iranian mythology. The struggle between Iran and Tūrān (the central Asian steppes from which new waves of nomadic conquerors distributed Iran's urban culture) forms the central theme of the book, and the importance of the legitimate succession of kings, who are endowed with royal charisma, is reflected throughout the composition. The poem contains very few Arabic words and is often considered the masterpiece of Persian national literature, although it lacks historical perspective. Its episodes have been the inspiration of miniaturists since the 14th century. Numerous attempts have been made to emulate it in Iran, India, and Turkey.

Other epic poems, on a variety of subjects, were composed during the 11th century. The first example is Asadī's (died *c.* 1072) didactic *Garshāsp-nāmeh* ("Book of Garshāsp"), whose hero is very similar to Rostam. The tales of Alexander and his journeys through foreign lands were another favourite topic.

Poetical romances were also being written at this time. They include the tale of *Varqeh o-Golshāh* ("Varqeh and Golshāh") by ʿEyyūqī (11th century) and *Vīs o-Rāmīn* ("Vīs and Rāmīn") by Fakhr od-Dīn Gorgānī (died after 1055), which has parallels with the Tristan story of European medieval romance. These were soon superseded, however, by the great romantic epics of Neẓāmī of Ganja (died *c.* 1209), in Caucasia. The latter are known as the *Khamseh* ("The Quintuplet" or "The Five") and, though the names of Vīs or Vāmeq continued for some time to serve as symbols of the longing lover, it was the poetical work of Neẓāmī that supplied subsequent writers with a rich store of images, similes, and stories to draw upon. The first work in his collection, *Makhzan ol-asrār* ("Treasury of Mysteries"), is didactic in intention. The subjects of the following three poems are traditional love stories. The first is the Arabic romance of Majnūn, who went mad with love for Laylā. Second is the Persian historical tale of Shīrīn, a Christian princess, loved by both the Sāsānian ruler Khosrow

This page comes from a 12th-century manuscript of the *Khamseh* of Neẓāmī. This particular manuscript is just one of many lavishly illustrated copies of the quintet of poems.

II Parvīz and the stonecutter Farhād. The third story, *Haft peykar* ("Seven Beauties"), deals with the adventures of Bahrām Gūr, a Sāsānian prince, and seven princesses, each connected with one day of the week, one particular star, one colour, one perfume, and so on. The last part of the *Khamseh* is *Eskandar-nāmeh*, which relates the adventures of Alexander the Great in Africa and Asia, as well as his discussions with the wise philosophers. It thus follows the traditions about Alexander and his tutor, Aristotle, emphasizing the importance of a counselor-philosopher in the service of a mighty emperor. Neẓāmī's ability to present a picture of life through highly refined language and a wholly apt choice of images is quite extraordinary. Human feelings, as he describes them, are fully believable; and his characters are drawn with a keen insight into human nature. Not surprisingly, Neẓāmī's work inspired countless poets' imitations in different languages—including Turkish, Kurdish, and Urdu—while painters illustrated his stories for centuries afterward.

Other Poetic Forms

In addition to epic poetry, the lesser forms, such as the *qaṣīdah* and *ghazal*, developed during the 11th and 12th centuries. Many poets wrote at the courts of the Seljuqs and also at the Ghaznavid court in Lahore, where the poet Masʿūd-e Saʿd-e Salmān (died 1121) composed a number of heartfelt *qaṣīdah*s during his political imprisonment. They are outstanding examples of the category of *ḥabsiyyah* (prison poem), which usually reveals more of the author's personal feelings than other literary forms. Other famous examples of *ḥabsiyyah*s include those written by the Arab knight Abū Firās (died 968) in a Byzantine prison; by Muḥammad II al-Muʿtamid of Sevilla (died 1095) in the dungeons of the Almohads; by the 12th-century Persian Khāqānī; by the Urdu poets Ghālib, in the 19th century, and Faiz, in the 20th; and by the modern Turkish poet Nazım Hikmet (died 1963).

The most-complicated forms were mastered by poets of the very early period, especially Qaṭrān, who was born near Tabrīz (now in Iran) and died after 1072. Through their display of virtuosity for virtuosity's sake, his *qaṣīdah*s reached the limits of artificiality. The court poets tried to top one another in the accumulation of complex metaphors and paradoxes, each hoping to win the coveted title "Prince of Poets." Anvarī (died *c.* 1189), whose patrons were the Seljuqs, is considered the most-accomplished writer of panegyrics in the Persian tongue. His verses contain little descriptive material but abound in learned allusions. His poem mourning the passing of Seljuq glory, famous in English as the *Tears of Khorāsān*, is among the best-known Persian *qaṣīdah*s.

In the west of Iran, Anvarī's contemporary Khāqānī (died *c.* 1190), who wrote mainly at the court of the Shīrvān-Shāhs of Transcaucasia, is the outstanding master of the hyperbolic style. His father was a Muslim, but his mother was a Nestorian Christian, and his imagery has more than the usual amount of allusions to Christian themes. His vocabulary seems inexhaustible; he uses uncommon rhetorical devices and very strong language. His poems are as impressive as his poignant antithetic formulations. Khāqānī's verses on the ruined Ṭāq Kisrā at Ctesiphon on the Tigris have become proverbial. His *qaṣīdah*s on the pilgrimage to Mecca, which also inspired his *mas̄nawī*, *Tuḥfat al-ʿIrāqayn* ("Gift of the Two Iraqs"), translate most eloquently the feelings of a Muslim at the festive occasion. In the hand of lesser poets, however, *qaṣīdah* writing became more and more conventionalized, repeating clichés and employing inflated terms devoid of feeling.

Scholarship: Al-Bīrūnī

The Ghaznavid and Seljuq periods produced first-rate scholars such as al-Bīrūnī (died 1048) who, writing in Arabic, investigated Hinduism and gave the first unprejudiced account of India—indeed, of any non-Islamic culture. He also wrote notable books on chronology and history. In his search for pure knowledge he is undoubtedly one of the greatest minds in Islamic history. Interest in philosophy is represented by Nāṣer-e Khusraw (died 1072/77), who acted for a time as a missionary for the Ismāʿīliyyah, a branch of Shīʿite Islam. His book about his journey to Egypt, entitled *Safar-nāmeh* (translated into English as *Diary of a Journey Through Syria and Palestine*), is a pleasing example of simple, clearly expressed, early Persian prose. His poetical works in the main seek to combine Greek wisdom and Islamic thought: the gnostic Ismāʿīlī interpretation of Islam seemed, to him, an ideal vehicle for a renaissance of the basic Islamic truths.

The encyclopaedic *The Chronology of Ancient Nations*, by Al-Bīrūnī, is devoted to a universal anthropological account of various cultures. This page is from a 15th-century manuscript of that work.

Omar Khayyam

The work done in mathematics by early Arabic scholars and by al-Bīrūnī was continued by Omar Khayyam (died 1131), to whom the Seljuq empire in fact owes the reform of its calendar. But Omar has become famous in the West through the very free adaptations by Edward FitzGerald of his *robāʿiyyāt*. These quatrains have been translated into almost every known language and are largely responsible for colouring European ideas about Persian poetry. Some scholars have doubted the authenticity of these verses. Since FitzGerald's time, many more faithful translations of the poems have been published.

The quatrain is an easy form to use—many have been scribbled on Persian pottery of the 13th century—and the same verse has been attributed to many authors. The latest research into the question of the *robāʿiyyāt* has established that a certain number of the quatrains can, indeed, be traced back to the great scientist who condensed in them his feelings and thoughts, his skepticism and love, in such an enthralling way that they appeal to every reader. The imagery he uses, however, is entirely inherited. One of the most noted, and notorious, writers of this genre was the female poet Mahsatī (first half of the 12th century), who frequently addressed members of different professions in rather frivolous lines. The quatrain was also popular as a means of embodying pieces of mystical wisdom. One has to do away with the old theory that the first author of such mystical *robāʿiyyāt* was Abū Saʿīd ibn Abū al-Khayr (died 1049). A number of his contemporaries, however, including Bābā Ṭāher ʿOryān (died after 1055), used simpler forms of the quatrain, sometimes in order to express their mystical concepts.

The great mathematician, astronomer, and poet Omar Khayyam was renowned in his own country and time mainly for his scientific achievements.

The Mystical Poem

Whereas the mystical thought stemming from Iran had formerly been written in Arabic, writers from the 11th century onward turned to Persian. Along with works of pious edification and theoretical discussions, what was to be one of the most common types of Persian literature came into existence: the mystical poem. Khwajah ʿAbd Allāh al-Anṣārī of Herāt (died 1088), a prolific writer on religious topics in both Arabic and Persian, first popularized the literary "prayer," or mystical contemplation, written in Persian in rhyming prose interspersed with verses. Sanāʾī (died 1131?), at one time a court poet of the Ghaznavids, composed the first mystical epic, the didactic *Ḥadīqat al-ḥaqīqat wa sharīʿat al-ṭariqah* ("The Garden of Truth and the Law of the Path"), which has some 10,000 verses. In this lengthy and rather dry poem, the pattern for all later mystical *mas̄navīs* is established: wisdom is embodied in stories and anecdotes; parables and proverbs are woven into the texture of the story, eventually leading back to the main subject, although the argument is without thread and the narration puzzling to follow. Among Sanāʾī's smaller *mas̄navīs*, *Sayr al-ʿibād ilā al-maʿād* ("The Journey of the Servants to the Place of Return") deserves special mention. Its theme is the journey of the spirit through the spheres, a subject dear to the mystics and still employed in modern times as, for example, by Iqbāl in his Persian *Jāvīd-nāmeh* (1932; "The Song of Eternity").

Sanāʾī's epic endeavours were continued by one of the most prolific writers in the Persian tongue, Farīd al-Dīn ʿAṭṭār (died *c.* 1220). He was a born storyteller, a fact that emerges from his lyrics but even more so from his works of edification. The most famous among his *mas̄navīs* is the *Manṭeq al-ṭayr* (*The Conference of the Birds*), modeled after some Arabic allegories. It is the story of 30 birds who, in search of their spiritual king, journey through seven valleys. The poem is full of tales, some of which have been translated even into the most remote Islamic languages. (The story of the pious Sheykh Ṣanʿān, who fell in love with a Christian maiden, is found, for example, in Kashmiri.) ʿAṭṭār's symbolism of the soul-bird was perfectly in accord with the existing body of imagery beloved of Persian poetry, but it was he who added a scene in which the birds eventually realize their own identity with God (because they, being *sī morgh*, or "30 birds," are identified with the mystical Sīmorgh, who represents God). Also notable are his *Elāhī-nāmeh* ("The Book of God"), an allegory of a king and his six sons, and his profound *Moṣībat-nāmeh* ("Book of Affliction"), which closes with its hero's being immersed in the ocean of his soul after wandering through the 40 stages of his search for God. The epic exteriorizes the mystic's experiences in the 40 days of seclusion.

Importance of Rūmī

The most famous of the Persian mystical *mas̄navī*s is by Jalāl al-Dīn al-Rūmī (died 1273) and is known simply as the *Mas̄navī*. It comprises some 26,000 verses and is a complete—though quite disorganized—encyclopaedia of all the mystical thought, theories, and images known in the 13th century. It is regarded by most of the Persian-reading orders of Sufis as second in importance only to the Qurʾān. Its translation into many Islamic languages and the countless commentaries written on it up to the present day indicate its importance in the formation of Islamic poetry and religious thought. Jalāl al-Dīn, who hailed from Balkh (in present-day Afghanistan) and settled in Konya (in present-day Turkey), the capital of the Rūm, or Anatolian Seljuqs (and hence was surnamed "Rūmī"), was also the author of love lyrics whose beauty surpasses even that of the tales in the *Mas̄navī*. Mystical love

Rūmī's *Mašnavī* widely influenced mystical thought and literature throughout the Muslim world. This page comes from a manuscript of the *Mašnavī* that was made in India *c.* 1663.

poetry had been written since the days of Sanāʾī, and theories of love had been explained in the most subtle prose and sensitive verses by the Sufis of the early 12th century. Yet Rūmī's experience of mystical love for the wandering mystic, Shams al-Dīn of Tabrīz, was so ardent and enraptured him to such an extent that he identified himself completely with Shams, going so far as to use the beloved's name as his own pen name. His dithyrambic lyrics, numbering more than 30,000 verses altogether, are not at all abstract or romantic. On the contrary, their vocabulary and imagery are taken directly from everyday life, so that they are vivid, fresh, and convincing. Often their rhythm invites the reader to partake in the mystical dance practiced by Rūmī's followers, the Mawlawiyyah (the name is derived from the honorific "Mawlānā"—meaning "Our Lord"—often bestowed on Rūmī). His verses sometimes approach the form of popular folk poetry. Indeed, Rūmī is reputed to have written mostly under inspiration, and, despite his remarkable poetical technique, the sincerity of his love and longing is never overshadowed, nor is his personality veiled. In these respects he is unique in Persian literature.

Zenith of Islamic Literature

During the 13th century the Islamic lands were exposed, on the political plane, to the onslaught of the Mongols and the abolition of the ʿAbbāsid caliphate, while vast areas were laid to waste. Yet this was in fact the period in which Islamic literatures reached their zenith. Apart from Rūmī's superb poetry, written in the comparative safety of Konya, there was also the work of the Egyptian Ibn al-Fāriḍ (died 1235), who composed some magnificent, delicately written mystical poems in *qaṣīdah* style, and that of Ibn al-ʿArabī, who composed love lyrics and numerous theosophical works that were to become standard.

In Iran one of the greatest literati, Saʿdī (died 1291), returned about 1256 to his birthplace, Shīrāz, after years of journeying, and his *Būstān* (*The Orchard*) and *Gulistān* (*The Rose Garden*) have been popular ever since. The *Būstān* is a didactic poem telling wise and uplifting moral tales, written in polished, easy-flowing style and a simple metre. The *Gulistān*, completed one year later, in 1258, has been judged "the finest flower that could blossom in a Sultan's garden" (Johann Gottfried von Herder). Its eight chapters deal with different aspects of human life and behaviour. At first sight its prose and poetical fragments appear to be simple and unassuming, but not a word could be changed without destroying the perfect harmony of the sound, imagery, and content. Saʿdī's *Gulistān* is thus essential in discovering the nature of the finest Persian literary style. Since the mid-17th century its moralizing stories have been translated into many Western languages. Saʿdī was likewise the author of some spirited *ghazal*s; he may have been the first writer in Iran to compose the sort of love poetry that is now thought of as characteristic of the *ghazal*. A few of his *qaṣīdah*s are also of note, although he is at his best in shorter forms. His elegant aphoristic poems, words of wisdom, and sensible advice all display what has been called the philosophy of common sense—how to act in any given situation so as to make the best of it both for oneself and others, basing one's conduct on the virtues of gentleness, elegance, modesty, and polite behaviour.

The influence of mysticism, on the one hand, and of the elaborate Persian poetical tradition, on the other, is apparent during the later decades of the 13th century, both in Anatolia and in Muslim India. The Persian mystic ʿIrāqī (died 1289), a master of delightful love lyrics, lived for almost 25 years in Multan (in present-day Pakistan), where his lively *ghazal*s are still sung. His short treatises, in a mixture

The blend of human kindness and cynicism, humour, and resignation displayed in Saʿdī's works makes him one of the most admired writers in the world of Iranian culture.

of poetry and prose (and written under Ibn al-ʿArabī's influence), have been imitated often.

While in Multan he may have met the young Amīr Khosrow of Delhi (died 1325), who was one of the most versatile authors to write in Persian, not only in India but in the entire realm of Persian culture. Amīr Khosrow, son of a Turkish officer but whose mother was Indian, is often styled, because of the sweetness of his speech, "the parrot of India." (In Persian, it should be noted, parrots are always "sugar-talking"; they are, moreover, connected with paradise and are thought of as wise birds—thus models of the sweet-voiced sage.) He wrote panegyrics of seven successive kings of Delhi and was also a pioneer of Indian Muslim music. Imitating Neẓāmī's *Khamseh*, Khosrow introduced a novelistic strain into the *mas̄navī* by recounting certain events of his own time in poetical form, some parts of which are lyrics. His style of lyrical poetry has been described as "powdered," and his *ghazal*s contain many of the elements that in the 16th and 17th centuries were to become characteristic of the "Indian" style. Khosrow's poetry surprises the reader in its use of unexpected forms and unusual images, complicated constructions and verbal plays, all handled fluently and presented in technically perfect language. His books on the art of letter writing prove his mastery of high-flown Persian prose. Khosrow's younger contemporary, Ḥasan of Delhi (died 1328), is less well known and had a more simple style. He nevertheless surpassed Khosrow in warmth and charm, qualities that earned him the title of "the Saʿdī of Hindustan."

Turkish Literature

As for the literary developments in Turkey about 1300, the mystical singer Yunus Emre is the first and most important in a long line of popular poets. Little is known about his life, which he probably spent not far from the Sakarya River of Asia Minor. Before him, in Central Asia, the religious leader Ahmed Yesevi (died 1166) had written some rather dry verses on wisdom in Turkish. Yunus, in Anatolia, however, was the first known poet to have caught something of Rūmī's fervour and translated it into a provincial setting, creating "a Turkish vernacular poetry that was to be the model for all subsequent literary productions of popular religion." Sometimes he used the inherited Arabo-Persian prosody, but his best poems are those written in four-line verses using syllable-counting metres. Yunus drew heavily on the reservoir of imagery that had been collected by the great Persian writing mystics, notably Rūmī, but his classical technique did not hinder the expression of his own unself-conscious simplicity, which led him to introduce new images taken from everyday life in Anatolian villages. His *ilahi*s (hymns), probably written to be sung at the meetings of the Sufis in the centres of their orders, are still loved by the Turks and memorized by their children.

Influence of Yunus Emre

The Turkish people rightly claim Yunus as the founder of Turkish literature proper. His poetry is considered the chief pillar of poetry of the Bektashi Sufi order, and many poets of this and other orders have imitated his style (though without reaching the same level of poetic truth and human warmth). Among the later poets claimed by the Bektashis may be mentioned Kaygusuz Abdal (15th century), who probably came from the European provinces of the Ottoman Empire. His verses are full of burlesque and even coarse images; in their odd mixture of worldliness and religious expression, they are often as amusing as they are puzzling. In the 16th century Pir Sultan Abdal (executed *c.* 1560) is noted for a few poems of austere melancholy. He was executed for collaboration with the Ṣafavids, the archenemies of the Ottomans, and in this connection it is worth remembering that the founder of the Iranian Ṣafavid dynasty, Shāh Ismāʿīl I (died 1524), wrote Turkish poetry under the pen name Khaṭāʾī and is counted among the Bektashi poets.

Religious Poetry

Mystically tinged poetry has always been very popular in Turkey, both in cities and in rural areas. The best-loved religious poem of all was, and still is, Süleyman Çelebi's (died 1419) *Mevlûd*, a quite short *mas̄navī* in honour of the Prophet Muhammad's birth. This type of poetry has been known in the Islamic countries since at least the 12th century and was soon adopted wherever Islam spread. There are a great number of *mevlûd* written in Turkish, but it was Süleyman Çelebi's unpretentious description of the great religious event that captured the hearts of the Turks, and it is still sung on many occasions (on the anniversary of a death, for example). The poem makes an excellent introduction to an understanding of the deep love for the Prophet felt by the pious Muslim.

Persian Literature: 1300–1500

In the Iran of the Middle Ages, a vast number of poets flourished at the numerous courts. Not only professional poets but even the kings and princes contributed more or less successfully to the body of Persian poetry. Epics, panegyrics, and mystico-didactical poetry had all reached their finest hour by the end of the 13th century; the one genre to attain perfection slightly later was the *ghazal*, of which Moḥammad Shams al-Dīn Ḥāfeẓ (died 1389/90) is the incontestable master.

Lyric Poetry

Ḥāfeẓ lived in Shīrāz; his pen name—"Who Knows the Qurʾān by Heart"—indicates his wide religious education, but little is known about the details of his life. The same is true of many Persian lyrical poets, because their products rarely contain much trustworthy biographical material. Ḥāfeẓ's comparatively small collection of work—his *Dīvān* contains about 400 *ghazal*s—was soon acclaimed as the finest lyrical poetry ever written in Persian. The discussion of whether or not to interpret its wine and love songs on a mystical plane has continued for centuries. Yet this discussion seems sterile since Ḥāfeẓ, whose verbal images shine like jewels, is an outstanding exponent of the ambiguous and oscillating style that makes Persian poetry so attractive and so difficult to translate.

The different levels of experience are all expressed through the same images and symbols: the beloved is always cruel, whether a chaste virgin (a rare case in Persian poetry!), a professional courtesan, a handsome young boy (in most cases), God (mysterious and unattainable), or even the remote despot, the wisdom of whose schemes must never be questioned by his subjects. Because mystical interpretation of the world order had become almost second nature to Persians during the 13th century, the human beloved could effortlessly be regarded as God's manifestation; the rose became a symbol of highest divine beauty and glory; the nightingale represented the yearning and complaining soul; wine, cup, and cupbearer became the embodiment of enrapturing divine love. The poets' multicoloured

قوام ملت و دین مجدالدین ابن علی   کمی درخشدش ازچهره فریزد ای

زهی حمیده خصالی دعوی جهانبانی

طراز دولت با نام عالم فا..ـیی

The great popularity of Ḥāfeẓ's poetry in all Persian-speaking lands stems from his simple though musical language and his unaffected use of homely images and proverbial expressions.

images were not merely decorative embroidery but were a structural part of their thought.

One must not expect Ḥāfeẓ (or any other poet) to unveil his personal feelings in a lyrical poem of experience. But no other Persian poet has used such complex imagery on so many different levels with such harmonious and well-balanced lucidity as did Ḥāfeẓ. His true greatness lies in this rather than in the content of his poetry. It must be stressed again that, according to the traditional view, each verse of a *ghazal* should be unique, precious for its own sake, and that the apparent lack of logic behind the sequence of verses was considered a virtue rather than a defect. (It may help to think of the glass pieces in a kaleidoscope, which appear in different patterns from moment to moment yet themselves form no logical pattern.) To what extent an "inner rhythm" and a "contrapuntal harmony" can be detected in Ḥāfeẓ's poetry is still a matter for discussion, but that he perfected the *ghazal* form is indisputable. Whether he is praised as a very human love poet, as an interpreter of esoteric lore, or as a political critic, his verses have a continuing appeal to all lovers of art and artistry.

Parodies of Classic Forms

Ḥāfeẓ's contemporary in Shīrāz was the satirist ʿObeyd-e Zākānī (died 1371), noted for his obscene verses (even the most moralistic and mystical poets sometimes produced surprisingly coarse and licentious lines) and for his short *mas̄navī* called *Mūsh o-gorbeh* ("Mouse and Cat"), an amusing political satire. Because few new forms or means of expression were open to them, ʿObeyd and other poets began ridiculing the classic models of literature; thus, Bosḥāq (died *c.* 1426) composed odes and *ghazal*s exclusively on the subject of food.

Jāmī's poetry is fresh and graceful and is not marred by unduly esoteric language. This illustration is from a 16th-century copy of his *Haft owrang*.

The Timurid period in Iran produced less original poetry, despite the rulers' interest in art. Allegorical *maṡnavī*s were much in vogue, such as the *Shabestān-e khayāl* ("Bedchamber of Fantasy") by the prolific writer Fattāḥī of Nīshāpūr (died 1448) and *Gūy o-chowgān* ("Ball and Polo-stick") by ʿĀrefī (died 1449); the latter work is an elaboration of the cliché that the lover is helpless before the will of his beloved, just as the ball is subject to the will of the polo-stick ("the head of the lover in the polo-stick of the beloved's tresses").

Eclecticism of ʿAbd al-Raḥmān Jāmī

The last great centre of Islamic art in the region of Iran was the Timurid court of Herāt, where Dowlatshāh (died 1494) composed his much-quoted biographical work on Persian poets. The leading figure in this circle was ʿAbd al-Raḥmān Jāmī (died 1492), who is sometimes considered the last and most comprehensive of the "seven masters" in Persian literature, because he was a master of every literary genre and did not specialize in one form only, as Anvarī and Ḥāfeẓ, among others, had done. Jāmī wrote an excellent imitation of Neẓāmī's *Khamseh*, enlarging it by the addition of two mystical *maṡnavī*s into a septet called *Haft owrang* ("The Seven Thrones," or "The Constellation of the Great Bear"). His interest in Sufism—he was initiated into the Naqshbandiyyah order—is clear from his famous biographies of the Sufi saints (which were an elaboration of a similar work by the 11th-century ʿAbd Allāh al-Anṣārī). In imitation of Saʿdī, Jāmī also composed the *Bahārestān* ("Orchard of Spring"), written in prose interspersed with verses. He left no less than three large divans, which contain work of high quality and demonstrate his gift for inventing picturesque images. Although his work abounds in lavishly ornamented verses, some have argued that his style on the whole lacks the perfect beauty of Ḥāfeẓ's lyrics and is already tending toward the heavier, more opaque "Indian" style. Jāmī also wrote treatises about literary riddles and various kinds of intellectual games, of which Muslim society in the late 15th century was very fond and which remain a feature of erudite Persian and Turkish poetry. His influence on the work of later poets, especially in Ottoman Turkey, was powerful.

An interesting aspect of the Timurid court in Herāt was the attention given to Chagatai Turkish, which was spoken in the eastern regions of Islam. ʿAlī Shīr Navāʾī, minister at the court (and a close friend of Jāmī), emphasized the beauties of his Turkic mother tongue as compared with Persian in his *Muḥākamat al-lughatayn* ("Judgment of the Two Languages"). He composed most of his lyrics and epics in Chagatai, which previously had been used by some members of the Timurid family and their courtiers for poetry but which became, thanks to him, an established literary medium. Even the arts-loving ruler of Herāt, Ḥusayn Bayqara (died 1506), wrote poetry in Turkic, following in every respect conventional literary taste.

Prose Works: The "Mirrors for Princes"

During the first five centuries of literature written in Modern Persian, a multitude of prose works were written. Among them the political instruction tradition known as "mirrors for princes" deserves special mention. This genre, introduced from Persian into Arabic as early as the 8th century, flourished once more in Iran during the late 11th century. One important example is the *Qābūs-nāmeh* ("The Book of Qābūs") by the Zeyārid prince ʿOnṣor ol-Maʿalī Keykāvūs (died 1098), which presents "a miscellany of Islamic culture in pre-Mongol times." At the same time, Niẓām al-Mulk (died 1092), the grand vizier of the Seljuqs, composed his *Seyāsat-nāmeh* (*The Book of Government* or *Rules for Kings*), a good introduction to the statesman's craft according to medieval Islamic standards. The *Seyāsat-nāmeh* was heavily influenced by pre-Islamic Persian tradition. In the same period and environment, even a mystic such as al-Ghazālī felt disposed to write a *Naṣīḥat al-mulūk* ("Counsel for Kings"), although the idealized relationship he makes between religious theory and practical statesmanship was not very realistic. A later mystic to compose a similar work was Sayyid ʿAlī Hamadhānī (died 1385), who had settled in Kashmir and initiated its Sufi poetry. Others, especially in India, exhorted rulers in their writings.

Belles Lettres

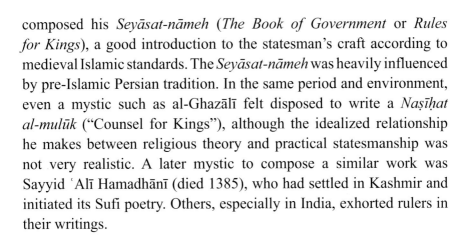

Belles lettres proper found a fertile soil in Iran. The fables of *Kalīlah wa Dimnah*, for example, were retold several times in Persian. The most famous version is called *Anvār-e soheylī* ("Lights of Canopus") and was composed by a famous mystic, Ḥoseyn Wāʿeẓ-e Kāshefī of Herāt (died 1504). The "cyclic story" form (in which several unconnected tales are held together by some device such as a common framework or narrator), inherited from India, became as popular in Iran as it had been in the Arabic-speaking countries. The *Sendbād-nāmeh* ("The Book of Sendbād [Sindbad]") and the *Ṭūṭī-nāmeh* ("Parrot Book"), which is based on Indian tales, are both good examples of the popular method whereby a variety of instructive stories are skillfully strung together within a basic "running" story. The first comprehensive collection of entertaining prose is *Jawāmīʿ al-ḥikayat* ("Collections of Stories"), a veritable storehouse of tales and anecdotes, by ʿOwfī (died *c.* 1230). Anecdotes were an important feature of the biographical literature that became popular in Iran and Muslim India. Biographies of the poets of a certain age or of a specified area were collected together. They provide the reader with few concrete facts about the subjects concerned, but they abound in anecdotes, sayings, and verses attributed to the subjects, thus preserving material that otherwise might have been lost. Many of these biographical manuals, such as ʿOwfī's *Lubāb al-albāb* ("Quintessence of the Hearts") or Dowlatshāh's *Tazkirat al-shuʿarā* ("Biography of the Poets"), make agreeable reading. The authors concerned wished to demonstrate their own erudition and rhetorical technique as much as to immortalize their subjects; consequently, their books are important equally as stylistic documents and as historical sources. One of the most-remarkable works in this field is *Chahār maqāleh* ("Four Treatises") by Neẓāmī-ye ʿArūẕī, a writer from eastern Iran. Written about 1156, this little book is an excellent introduction to the ideals of Persian literature and its writers, discussing in detail what is required to make a perfect poet, giving a number of instances of the sort of poetic craftsmanship thought especially admirable, and allowing glimpses into the various arts in which the literary man was expected to excel.

This tendency toward "anecdotal" writing, which is also manifest in the work of a number of Arab historians, can be observed in the cosmographic books and in some of the historical books produced in medieval Iran. The cosmography of Ḥamdollāh Mostowfī (died after 1340), *Nuzhat al-qulūb* ("Pleasure of the Hearts"), like many earlier works of this genre, underlined the mysterious aspects of the marvels of creation and was the most famous of several instructive collections of mixed folkloristic and scientific material. Early miniaturists, too, loved to illustrate the most unlikely tales and pieces of information given in such works. Historical writing proper had been begun by the Persians as early as the late 10th century, when Balʿamī made an abridged translation of the vast Arabic historical chronicle by al-Ṭabarī (died 923).

The heyday of historiography in Iran, however, was the Il-Khanid period (mid-13th to mid-14th century). Iran was then ruled by the successors of Genghis (Chinggis) Khan, and scholars began to extend their interest back to the history of pre-Islamic Central Asia, whence the rulers had come. *Tārīkh-e jehān-goshāy* ("History of the World Conqueror") by ʿAṭā Malek Joveynī (died 1283) and *Jāmiʿ al-tawārīkh* ("Collector of Chronicles") by the physician and vizier Rashīd al-Dīn (executed 1318) are both outstanding examples of histories filled with valuable information. Although the writing of history became a firmly established art in Iran and the adjacent Muslim countries, the facts were often concealed in a bombastic style and a labyrinth of long-winded sentences. A history written by Vaṣṣāf (died 1323) is the most notorious example of turgidity, but even his style was surpassed by some later writers. These stylistic tendencies deeply influenced Turkish prose writing: 17th-century Turkish historical works, such as those of Peçevi (died *c.* 1650) and Naima (died 1716), for this reason almost defy translation. This development in Persian and Turkish prose is also reflected in the handbooks on style and letter writing that were written during the 14th and 15th centuries and afterward. They urged the practice of all the tricks of rhetoric by this time considered essential for an elegant piece of prose.

Popular Literature

Islamic literatures should not be thought to consist only of erudite and witty court poetry, of frivolous or melancholy love lyrics full of literary conceits, or of works deeply mystical in content. Such works are counterbalanced by a great quantity of popular literature, of which the most famous expression is *Alf laylah wa laylah* (*The Thousand and One Nights*, also known as *The Arabian Nights' Entertainment*).

The tales collected under this title come from different cultural areas; their nucleus is of Indian origin, first translated into Persian as *Hazār afsānak* ("Thousand Tales") and then into Arabic. These fanciful fairy tales were later expanded with stories and anecdotes from Baghdad. Subsequently some tales—mainly from the lower strata of society—about rogues, tricksters, and vagabonds were added in Egypt. Independent series of stories, such as that of Sindbad the Sailor, were also included. The entire collection is very important as a reflection of several aspects of Middle Eastern folklore and allows, now and then, glimpses into the court life of the various dynasties. Since its first translation into French (1704) and for the better part of three centuries, it fed a romantic notion in the West regarding the Middle East.

From pre-Islamic times the Arabs had recounted tales of the *ayyām al-ʿArab* ("Days of the Arabs"), which were stories of their tribal wars, and had dwelt upon tales of the heroic deeds of certain of their brave warriors, such as ʿAntarah. Modern research, however, suggests that his story in its present setting belongs to the period of the Crusades. The Egyptian queen Shajar al-Durr (died 1250) and the first brave Mamlūk ruler, Baybars I (died 1277), as well as the adventures of the Bedouin tribe Banū Hilāl on its way to Tunisia, are all the subjects of lengthy popular tales.

In Iran many of the historical legends and myths had been borrowed and turned into high literature by Ferdowsī. Accounts of the glorious adventures of heroes from early Islamic times were afterward retold throughout Iran, India, and Turkey. Thus, the *Dāstān-e Amīr Ḥamzeh*, a story of Muhammad's uncle Ḥamzah ibn ʿAbd al-Muṭṭalib, was slowly enlarged by the addition of more and more fantastic details. This form of *dāstān*, as such literature is called, to some extent influenced the first attempts at novel writing in Muslim India during the 19th century. The epics of Köroğlu are common to both Iranian

Ali Baba's son, who one day invited him to his father's house. On hearing that the new guest would eat no salt with his meat, Morgiana's suspicions were aroused, and she recognised him as the captain of the robbers. After dinner she undertook to perform a dance before the company, and at the end of it pointed a dagger at the captain, and then plunged it into his heart. Ali Baba was very much shocked, until Morgiana explained the reasons for her conduct; he then gave her to his son in marriage, and they lived in great prosperity and happiness ever after.

The Thousand and One Nights became well known even outside the Islamic world. This illustration of one of the stories is by the English artist Walter Crane and dates from 1873.

and Turkish tradition. He was a noble warrior-robber who became one of the central figures in folk literature from Central Asia to Anatolia.

Some popular epics were composed in the late Middle Ages and were based on local traditions. One such epic had as its basis the Turco-Iranian legend of an 8th-century hero, Abū Muslim, another the Turkish tales of the knight Dānishmend. Other epics, such as the traditional Turkish tale of Dede Korkut, were preserved by storytellers who improvised certain parts of their tales (which were written down only afterward). Also, the role of the Sufi orders and of the artisans' lodges in preserving and transmitting such semihistorical popular epics seems to have been considerable. Apart from heroic figures, the Muslim peoples further share a comic character—basically a type of low-class theologian, called Nasreddin Hoca in Turkish, Juḥā in Arabic, and Mushfiqī in Tajik. Anecdotes about this character, which embody the mixture of silliness and shrewdness displayed by this "type," have amused generations of Muslims.

Shortly after the introduction of the printing press, Turkey and Iran began to produce cheap books, sometimes illustrated, containing popular romantic love stories. Large numbers of fairy tales were published in these cheap editions, and still other fairy tales were collected by European and Muslim folklorists.

A truly popular poetry is everywhere to be found: lullabies sung by mothers around the world have obvious similarities; workers sing little rhythmical poems to accompany their work; and nomads remember the adventures of their ancestors in their ballads. Such popular poems often contain dialect forms, and the metres differ from the classical quantitative system. Some of these simple verses, such as a two-line *lanḍay* in Pashto, are among the most graceful products of Islamic poetry. Many folk songs—lullabies, wedding songs, and dirges—have a distinct mystical flavour and reflect the simple Muslim's love for the Prophet and trust in God's grace even under the most difficult circumstances. Irony and wit are features of the riddle poem, a favourite form among Muslims everywhere. Folk poets were also fond of humorous descriptions of imaginary disputes between two entities—they might compose dialogues between coffee and tobacco (Morocco), between a big and a small mosque (Yemen), between a cat and a dog, or between a boy and a girl. All the Iranian and Turkic languages, too, possess a rich heritage of popular poetry, which in many cases appeals more immediately to modern tastes than does the rather cerebral high literature of the urban and court cultures.

CHAPTER 6

THE PERIOD FROM 1500 TO 1800

According to Persian tradition, the last classic author in literature was Jāmī, who died in 1492. In that year Christopher Columbus set off on his first transatlantic voyage, and the Christians reconquered Granada, the last Moorish stronghold of Spain. The beginning of the 16th century was as crucial in the history of the Muslim East as in the history of the Western Hemisphere. In 1501 the young Ismāʿīl founded the Ṣafavid rule in Iran, and the Shīʿite persuasion of Islam was declared the state religion. At the same time, the kingdoms of the last Timurid rulers in Central Asia were overthrown by the Uzbeks, who, for a while, tried to continue the cultural tradition in both Persian and Turkic at their courts in Bukhara. In 1526, after long struggles, one member of the Timurid house, Bābur, laid the foundation of the Mughal Empire in India. In the Middle East the Ottoman Turks, having expanded their empire (beginning in the late 13th century) from northwestern Anatolia into the Balkans, conquered crumbling Mamlūk Egypt and adjacent countries, including the sacred places of Mecca and Medina in 1516–17. Thus, three main blocks emerged, and the two strongholds of Sunni Islam—Ottoman Turkey and Mughal India—were separated by Shīʿite Iran.

پرتافته بهندوستان رى ودخیال نموده یکے بلى نیان دشته
خوبان ایشان هم بهدى کشتند بانجا رسید که صباحى که از
جیکدالیک کوچ مى نمودیم افغانانى که در میان بو دند مثل
خضرخل وشموخیل وخزلطى وخوکیانى خیال ببتن راه کوتل
جیکدالیک نموده برکوسى که بطرف شمال است راست
کرد آمده و دهها نوا اخته وشمشیر بازى کرده تبکه تبکه کردن
کردن گرفتند مجرد پیواریشدن فرمودم که مردم لشکر هرکس از
طرف خود برکوه برآیند مردم لشکر از سردره وسرطرف یافته

This page from Bābur's memoir, the
Bābur-nāmeh, shows the ruler marching
from Kabul to Hindustan. Written in
the Chagatai language, it was later
translated into Persian.

DECENTRALIZATION OF ISLAMIC LITERATURES

Ṣafavid Iran, as it happened, lost most of its artists and poets to the neighbouring countries. There were no great masters of poetry in Iran between the 16th and 18th centuries. And while the Persian shah Ismāʿīl I wrote Turkish mystical verses, his contemporary and enemy, Sultan Selim I of Turkey (died 1520), composed quite elegant Persian *ghazal*s. Bābur (died 1530), in turn, composed his autobiography in Eastern Turkic.

Bābur's autobiography is a fascinating piece of Turkish prose and at the same time one of the comparatively rare examples of Islamic autobiographical literature. The classic example in this genre, however, was a lively Arabic autobiography by Usāmah ibn Munqidh (died 1188), which sheds much light upon the life and cultural background of a Syrian knight during the Crusades. A number of mystics, too, had written their spiritual autobiographies in a variety of languages, with varying degrees of artistic success. Bābur's book, however, gives a wonderful insight into the character of this intrepid conqueror. It reveals him as a master of concise matter-of-fact prose, as a keen observer of daily life, full of pragmatic common sense, and also as a good judge of poetry. Bābur even went so far as to write a treatise in Turkish about versification. Many of his descendants, both male and female, inherited his literary taste and talent for poetry; among them are remarkably good poets in Persian, Turkish, and Urdu, as well as accomplished authors of autobiographies (Jahāngīr) and letters (Aurangzeb). Among the nobility of India, the Turkish language remained in use until the 19th century. Lovely Turkish verses were written, for example, by Akbar's general, ʿAbd al-Raḥīm Khān-e Khānān (died 1626), who was a great patron of fine arts and poetry.

In the Arab world there was hardly a poet or original writer of note during the three centuries that followed the Ottoman conquest, apart from some theologians (ʿAbd al-Wahhāb al-Shaʿrānī, died 1565; ʿAbd al-Ghanī al-Nābulusī, died 1731) and grammarians. Yet Arabic still remained the language of theology and scholarship throughout the Muslim world; both Turkey and India could boast a large number of scholars who excelled in the sacred language. In Ottoman Turkey, Taşköprüzade (died 1560) compiled a historical survey of outstanding Turkish intellectuals in Arabic. Although a fine example of Islamic learning, in usefulness it does not compare to the bibliographic work in Arabic by Hacı Halifa (Kâtip Çelebi; died 1658), which is a valuable source for modern knowledge of literary history.

NEW IMPORTANCE OF INDIAN LITERATURE

India's share in the development of Arabic literature at this time was especially large. In addition to the quantity of theological work written in the language of the Qurʾān, from the conquest of Sindh (in present-day Pakistan) in 711 right up until the 19th century, much philosophical and biographical literature in Arabic was also being written in the subcontinent. Persian taste predominated in the northwest of India, but in the southern provinces there were long-standing commercial and cultural relationships with the Arabs, especially in Yemen and Ḥaḍramawt, and an inclination toward preserving these intact. Thus, much poetry in conventional Arabic style was written during the 16th and 17th centuries, mainly in the kingdom of Golconda. There are even attempts at the epic form. A century after the heyday of Arabic in the Deccan, Āzād Bilgrami (died 1786) composed numerous poetical and biographical works in Persian, but his chief fame was as the "Ḥassān of Hind," since he, like the Prophet Muhammad's

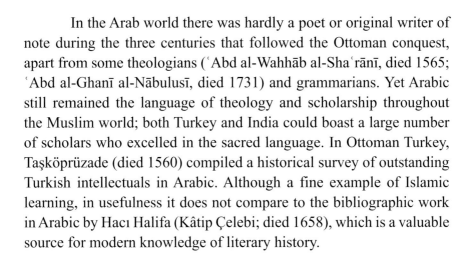

India's rich literary tradition was an influence in the Mughal period. This image comes from a copy of a Hindu text, the *Mahabharata*, that was made for the Mughal emperor Akbar.

protégé Ḥassān ibn Thābit, wrote some powerful Arabic panegyrics in honour of the Prophet. He even attempted to make a comparison of the characteristics of Arabic and Sanskrit poetry and tried to prove that India was the real homeland of Islam. It should be added that al-Sayyid Murtaḍā al-Zabīd (died 1791), a leading philologist, author of the fundamental work of lexicography *Tāj al-ʿarūs* ("The Bride's Crown"), and commentator on Ghazālī's main work, was of Indian origin. Laudatory poems and belles lettres in Arabic were still popular in the early 19th century at the Shīʿite court of Lucknow, then the chief centre of Urdu poetry.

Nevertheless, the main contribution of Muslim India to high literature was made in the Persian tongue. Persian had been the official language of the country for many centuries. The numerous annals and chronicles that were compiled during the 14th and 15th centuries, as well as the court poetry, had been composed exclusively in this language even by Hindus. During the Mughal period its importance was enhanced both by Akbar's attempt to have the main works of classical Sanskrit literature translated into Persian and by the constant influx of poets from Iran who came seeking their fortune at the lavish tables of the Indian Muslim grandees. At this time what is known as the "Indian" style of Persian emerged. The translations from Sanskrit enriched the Persian vocabulary, and new stories of Indian origin added to the reservoir of classical imagery. The poets, bound to the inherited genres of *maṡnavī*, *qaṣīdah*, and *ghazal*, tried to outdo each other in the use of complex rhyme patterns and unfamiliar, often stiff, metres. It became fashionable to conceive a poem according to a given *zamīn* ("ground"), in emulation of a classical model, and then to enrich it with newly invented tropes. The long-held ideal of "harmonious selection of images" was not always met. Difficult, even awkward grammatical constructions and inverted metaphors can be found. At times, pseudo-philosophical utterances in the second hemistich of a verse contrast strangely with semicolloquial expressions elsewhere. Objects recently introduced to India, such as the eyeglass or hourglass, were eagerly adopted as images by the poets, who wanted newfangled conceits to bolster their tortuous inventiveness. Notwithstanding the colourful descriptive poems written in praise of such subjects as Mughal palaces, marvelously illuminated manuscripts, rare elephants, or court scenes, the general mood of lyric poetry became more gloomy. The transitory nature of the world, also a central theme in classical Persian poetry, was stressed and depicted in bizarre images: "burnt nest," "breakdown," "yawning" (indicating insatiable thirst); these were some of the new "stylish" words.

Yet some truly great poets are to be found even in this period. ʿUrfī, who left Shīrāz for India and died in his mid-30s in Lahore (1592), is without doubt one of the genuine masters of Persian poetry, especially in his *qaṣīdah*s. His verses pile up linguistic difficulties, yet their dark, glowing quality cannot fail to touch the hearts and minds even of critical modern readers—more so than the elegant but rather cerebral verses of his colleague Fayzī (died 1595), one of Akbar's favourites. Fayzī's brother Abū-ul-Fazī ʿAllāmī (died 1602), the author of an important, though biased, historical work, deeply influenced the emperor's religious ideas. Among 17th-century Mughal court poets, the most outstanding is Abū Ṭālib Kalīm (died 1651), who came from Hamadan. Abounding in descriptive passages of great virtuosity, his poignant and often pessimistic verses have become proverbial, thanks to their compact diction and fluent style. Also of some importance is Ṣāʾib of Tabriz (died 1677), who spent only a few years in India before returning to Iran. Yet, of his immense poetical output (300,000 couplets), the great majority belongs to the stock-in-trade expression of the Persian-speaking world. Other poets described the lives and adventures of members of the royal families, usually in verbose *mas̄navī*s (this kind of descriptive historical poetry was practiced throughout Muslim India and also in Ottoman Turkey). Outside the Mughal environment, the lyrics and *mas̄navī*s by Ẓuhūrī (died 1615) at the court of Bijāpur are notably charming and enjoyable.

The heir apparent of the Mughal Empire, Dārā Shikōh (executed 1659), also followed Akbar's path. His inclination to mysticism is reflected in both his prose and poetry. The Persian translation of the *Upanishad*s, which he sponsored (and in part wrote himself), enriched Persian religious prose and made a deep impression on European idealistic philosophy in the 19th century. A group of interesting poets gathered about him, none of them acceptable to orthodoxy. They included the convert Persian Jew Sarmad (executed 1661), author of mystical *robāʿiyyāt*, and the Hindu Brahman (died

PASHTO POETRY

From the borderlands of the Persian-speaking zone, culturally under Mughal rule, one poet deserves special attention. The chief of the Pashtun tribe of Khaṭak, Khushḥāl Khān (died 1689), rightly deserves to be called the father of Pashto poetry, for he virtually created a literature of his own in his mother tongue. His skill in translating the sophisticated traditions of Persian literature into the not too highly developed idiom of the Pashtuns is astonishing. His lively lyric poems are his finest works, reflecting that passionate love of freedom for which he fought against the Mughals. The poems he wrote from prison in "hell-like hot India" are as dramatic as they are touching in their directness. Many members of his family took to poetry, and during the 18th century original works, both religious and secular, were composed in Pashto, and the classics of Persian literature were translated into that language.

1662), whose prose work *Chahār chaman* ("Four Meadows") gives an interesting insight into life at court.

With the long rule of Dārā Shikōh's brother, the austere Aurangzeb (died 1707), the heyday of both poetry and historical writing in Muslim India was over. Once more, orthodox religious literature gained preeminence, while poets tried to escape into a fantasy world of dreams. The style of the two leading poets of this age, Nāṣir ʿAlī Sirhindī (died 1697) and Mīrzā Bēdil (died 1721), is convoluted and obscure, prompting the Persian poet Ḥazīn (died 1766), who went to India in the early 18th century, to write ironic comments about its incomprehensibility.

Bēdil, however, was a very interesting writer. His lyric poetry is difficult but often rewarding, while his many philosophical *mas̄navī*s deserve deep study. His prose work, interspersed with poetry, is called *Chahār ʿunṣur* ("Four Elements") and contains some biographical details. His prose is nearly as difficult as his poetry, and, consequently, Bēdil's works rarely have been read outside of India. His poetry, however, has had a great influence in Afghanistan and Central Asia. Many Persian-speaking people there consider him the forerunner of Tajik literature, because virtually everyone in Bukhara and Transoxania who tried to write poetry knew and followed Bēdil's example. His ideas, sometimes astoundingly modern and progressive, also impressed the great 20th-century poet and philosopher Muḥammad Iqbāl in what is now Pakistan.

With Bēdil the "Indian summer" of Persian literature came to an end, even though the output of Persian poetry and prose during the 18th century in the subcontinent was immense. Some of the biographical dictionaries and handbooks of mysticism are valuable for the scholar but are less interesting as part of the general history of literature. The main vehicle of poetry became the Urdu language, while mystical poetry flourished in Sindhi and Punjabi.

OTTOMAN TURKEY

The development of literature in Ottoman Turkey is almost parallel with that of Iran and India. Yunus Emre had introduced a popular form of mystical poetry, yet the mainstream of secular and religious literature followed Persian models (although it took some time to establish the Persian rules of prosody, because of the entirely different structure of the Turkish language). In the religious field, the vigour and boldness expressed in the poems of Seyyid ʿImād al-Dīn Nesīmī (executed *c.* 1418) left their traces in the work of later poets, none of whom, however, reached his loftiness and grandeur of expression. The 14th- and 15th-century representatives of the classical style displayed great charm in their literary compositions, their verses simple and pleasing. Sultan Cem (Jem; died 1495), son of Mehmed the Conqueror, is an outstanding representative of their number. But soon the high-flown style of post-classical Persian was being imitated by Ottoman authors, rhetoric often being more important to them than poetical content. The work of Bâkî (Bāqī; died 1600) is representative of the entire range of those baroque products. Yet his breathtaking command of language is undeniable; it is brilliantly displayed in his elegy on Süleyman the Magnificent. In his time, according to a popular saying, one could find "a poet under every stone of Istanbul's pavement." Istanbul was the unique cultural centre of the Middle East, praised throughout the ages by all who lived in the imperial city.

POETRY OF FUZULI OF BAGHDAD

Much greater than most of these minor poets, however, was a writer living outside the capital, Fuzuli of Baghdad (died 1556), who wrote

This illustration from Fuzuli of Baghdad's *Hadiqat al-Suʿada* (*Garden of the Blessed*) shows Abraham being cast into the fire. Fuzuli's works influenced many poets up to the 19th century.

in Arabic, Persian, and Azeri Turkish. Apart from his lyrics, his Turkish *mas̄navī* on the traditional subject of the lovers Majnūn and Laylā is admirable. From earliest times, Turkish poets had emulated the classical Persian romantic *mas̄navī*s, sometimes surpassing their models in expressiveness. Fuzuli's diction is taut, his command of imagery masterful. His style unfortunately defies poetical translation, and his complicated fabric of plain and inverted images, of hidden and overt allusions, is well-nigh impossible for all but the initiated Muslim reader to disentangle. Fuzuli, moreover, like his fellow poets, would blend Arabic, Persian, and Turkish constructions and words to make up a multifaceted unit. The same difficulty is found in Turkish prose literature of the same period. It is a major task to unravel the long trailing sentences of a writer such as Evliya Çelebi (died *c.*1684), who, in an account of his travels (*Seyahatname*), has left extremely valuable information about the cultural climate in different parts of the Ottoman Empire.

LATER DEVELOPMENTS

Growing interest in the Indo-Persian style, particularly in ʿUrfī's *qaṣīdah*s, led the 17th-century Ottoman poets to a new integrated style and precision of diction. An outstanding representative was Nefʿi, whose bent for merciless satire made him dreaded in the capital and eventually led to his assassination. At the start of the 18th century, a marked but short-lived movement in Turkish art known as the "Tulip Period" was the Ottoman counterpart of European Rococo. The musical poems and smooth *ghazal*s of Ahmed Nedim (died 1730) reflect the manners and style of the slightly decadent, relaxed, and at times licentious high society of Istanbul and complement the miniatures of his contemporary Abdülcelil Levnî (died 1732). Good

Turkish poetry is characterized by an easy grace, to be found even in such mystically tinged poems (thousands of which were written throughout the centuries) as those of Niyazî Misrî (died 1697). The Mevlevî (Mawlawī) poet Gâlib Dede (died 1799) was already standing at the threshold of what can now be recognized as modern poetical expression in some of the lyrical parts of his *mas̄navī*, called *Hüsn ü aşk* ("Beauty and Love"), which brought fresh treatment to a well-worn subject of Iran's philosophical and secular literature. His work cannot be properly understood, however, without a thorough knowledge of mystical psychology, expressed in multivalent images.

FOLK POETRY

One branch of literature, however, was totally neglected by the sophisticated inhabitants of the Ottoman capital. Nobody thought much of the folk poets who wandered through the forgotten villages of Anatolia singing in simple syllable-counting verses of love, longing, and separation. The poems of the mid-17th-century figure Karacaoğlan, one of the few historically datable folk poets, give a vivid picture of village life, of the plight of girls and boys in remote Anatolian settlements. This kind of poetry was rediscovered only after the foundation of the Turkish Republic in 1923 and then became an important influence on modern lyric poetry.

CHAPTER 7

The Emergence of Western Forms

For the Islamic countries, the 19th century marks the beginning of a new epoch. Napoleon's conquest of Egypt, as well as British colonialism, brought the Muslims into contact with a world whose technology was far in advance of their own. The West had experienced the Renaissance, the Reformation, and the Enlightenment, whereas the once-flourishing Muslim civilization had experienced less change and innovation despite its remarkable artistic achievements. The introduction of Muslim intellectuals to Western literature and scholarship—the Egyptian al-Ṭahṭāwī (died 1873), for example, studied in France—ushered in a new literary era the chief characteristic of which was to be "more matter, less art." The literatures from this time onward are far less "Islamic" than those of the previous 1,000 years, but new intellectual experiences also led to "the liberation of the whole creative impulse within the Islamic peoples" (as argued by James Kritzeck, an American scholar of Islam). The introduction of the printing press and the expansion of newspapers helped to shape a new literary style, more in line with the requirements of modern times, when, as one scholar put it, "the patron prince has been replaced by a middle-class reading public."

Translations from Western languages provided writers with the model examples of genres previously unknown to them, including the novel, the short story, and dramatic literature. Of

Amīr Shakīb Arslān became one of the leading figures in the Islamic world between the first and second world wars. He is probably best known for his book ***Our Decline: Its Causes and Remedies***. He also established the journal ***La Nation Arabe***.

those authors whose books were translated, Guy de Maupassant, Sir Walter Scott, and Anton Chekhov were most influential in the development of the novel and the novella. Important also was the ideological platform derived from Leo Tolstoy, whose criticism of Western Christianity was gratefully adopted by writers from Egypt to Muslim India. Western influences can further be observed in the gradual discarding of the time-hallowed static style of both poetry and prose, in the tendency toward simplification of diction, and in the adaptation of syntax and vocabulary to meet the technical demands of emulating Western models.

Contact with the West also encouraged a tendency toward retrospection. Writers concentrated their attention on their own country and particular heritage, such as the "pharaoic myth" of Egypt, the Indo-European roots of Iran, and the Central Asian past of Turkey. In short, there was an emphasis on differentiation, inevitably leading to the rise of nationalism, instead of an emphasis on the unifying spirit and heritage of Islam.

ARAB LITERATURES

Given this situation, the heralds of Arab nationalism (as reflected in literature) were Christians. The historical novels of Jurjī Zaydān (died 1914), a Lebanese living in Egypt, made a deep impression on younger writers by glorifying the lionhearted national heroes of past times. Henceforth, the historical novel was to be a favourite genre in all Islamic countries, including Muslim India. The inherited tradition of the heroic or romantic epic and folktale was blended with novelistic techniques learned from Sir Walter Scott. Two writers in the front rank of Arab intellectuals were Amīr Shakīb Arslān (died 1946), of Druze origin, and Muḥammad Kurd ʿAlī (died 1953), the founder of the Arab Academy of Damascus, each of whom, by encouraging a new degree of awareness, made an important contribution to the education of modern historians and persons of letters. An inclination toward Romanticism can be detected in prose writing but not, surprisingly, in poetry; thus, the Egyptian Muṣṭafā Luṭfī al-Manfalūṭī (died 1924) poured out his feelings in a number of novels that touch on Islamic as well as national issues.

Poetry

It is fair to say of this transition period that the poetry being written was not as interesting as the prose. The *qaṣīdah*s of the "Prince of Poets," Aḥmad Shawqī (died 1932), are for the most part ornate works based on the classical models. Even the "Poet of the Nile," Ḥāfiẓ Ibrāhīm (died 1932), who was more interested in the real problems of the day, was nonetheless content to follow conventional patterns. In his poems, Khalīl Muṭrān (died 1949) attempted to achieve a unity of structure hitherto almost unknown, and he also adopted a more subjective approach to expressive lyricism. Thus, he can be said to have inaugurated an era of "Romantic" poetry, staunchly defended by those writers and scholars who had come under English rather than French influence. These included the poet and essayist Ibrāhīm al-Māzinī (died 1949) and the prolific writer of poetry and prose ʿAbbās Maḥmūd al-ʿAqqād (died 1964).

Prose

A major contribution to the development of modern prose in the Arabic language was made by a number of writers born between 1889 and 1902. One of them, the "humanist" Ṭāhā Ḥusayn, became well known

THE DIASPORA

A considerable amount of Arabic literature was produced during the 20th century by numerous writers who settled in non-Islamic countries, especially in the United States and Brazil. Most of these writers came from Christian Lebanese families. A feeling of nostalgia often led them to form literary circles or launch magazines or newspapers. The Arabic-language newspaper *Al-Hudā* (or *Al-Hoda*, "The Guidance"), established in 1898, was published in New York City as *Al-Hudā al-jadīdah* (*Al-Hoda Aljadidah*; "The New Al-Hoda," or "The New Guidance"). It was largely because of their work that the techniques of modern fiction and modern free verse entered Arabic literature and became a decisive factor in it.

One of the best-known authors in this group was Ameen Rihani (died 1941), whose descriptions of his journeys through the Arab world are informative and make agreeable reading. The fact that so many Lebanese emigrated led to the creation of a standard theme in Lebanese fiction: emigrants returning to their villages. Modern Iraqi literature is best represented by "the poet of freedom" Maʿrūf al-Ruṣāfī (died 1945), and Jamīl Sidqī al-Zahāwī (died 1936), whose satire *Thawrah fī al-Jaḥīm* ("Rebellion in Hell") incurred the wrath of the traditionalists.

in the West as a literary critic who attacked the historical authenticity of pre-Islamic poetry and stressed the importance of Greek and Latin for the literatures of the modern Middle East. He was also the author of a successful novel called *The Tree of Misery*, but his best creative writing is in his fictionalized autobiography, *Al-Ayyām* (1929–67; *The Days*), the three parts of which describe in simple language the life of a blind Egyptian village boy. Ṭāhā Ḥusayn's generation became more and more absorbed by the problems of the middle classes (to which most of them belonged), and this led them to realism in fiction. Some turned to fierce social criticism, depicting in their writings the dark side of everyday life in Egypt and elsewhere. The leading writer of this group was Maḥmūd Taymūr, who wrote short stories, a genre developed in Arabic by a Lebanese Christian who settled in the United States, the noted and versatile poet Khalil Gibran (died 1931). Muḥammad Ḥusayn Haykal (died 1956), a leading figure of Egyptian cultural and political life and the author of numerous historical studies, touched on the difficulties of Egyptian villagers for the first time, in his novel *Zaynab* (1913). This subject became fashionable quickly afterward, although not all the writers had firsthand knowledge of the feelings and problems of the fellahin. The most fertile author of this group was al-ʿAqqād, who tirelessly produced biographies, literary criticism, and romantic poetry. The Islamic reform movement led by Muḥammad ʿAbduh (died 1905) and his disciples, which centred on the journal *Al-Manār* ("The Lighthouse"), influenced Arabic prose style across the 20th century and was important in shaping the religious outlook of many authors writing in the 1920s and '30s.

TURKISH LITERATURES

The same changing attitude toward the function of literature and the same shift toward realism can be observed in Turkey. After 1839, Western ideas and forms were taken up by a group of modernists. Ziya Paşa (died 1880), the translator of Jean-Jacques Rousseau's *Émile* (which became a popular textbook for 19th-century Muslim intellectuals), was among the first to write in a less traditional idiom and to complain in his poetry—just as Ḥālī was to do in India a few years later—about the pitiable conditions of Muslims under the victorious Christians. Ziya Paşa, together with İbrahim Şinasi (died 1871) and Namık Kemal (died 1888), founded an influential Turkish journal, *Tasvir-i Efkâr* ("Picture of Ideas"). The essential theme of the articles, novels, poems, and dramas composed by these authors is their fatherland (*vatan*), and they dared to advocate freedom of thought, democracy, and constitutionalism. Abdülhak Hâmid (died 1935), though considerably their junior, shared in their activities. In 1879 he published his epoch-making *Sahra* ("The Country"), a collection of 10 Turkish poems that were the first to be composed in Western verse forms and style. Later he turned to unusual and often morbid subject matter in his poetic dramas. He, like his colleagues, had to endure political restrictions on writing, imposed as part of the harsh measures taken by Sultan Abdülhamid II against the least sign of liberal thought. Influenced by his work, later writers aimed to simplify literary language: Ziya Gökalp (died 1924) laid the philosophical foundations of Turkish nationalism; and Mehmed Emin, a fisherman's son, sang artless Turkish verses of his pride in being a Turk, throwing out the heavy rhetorical ballast of Arabo-Persian prosody and instead turning to the language of the people, unadulterated by any foreign vocabulary. The stirrings of social criticism could be discerned after 1907. Mehmed Akif (died 1936), in his masterly narrative poems, gave a vivid critical picture of conditions in Turkey before World War I. His powerful and dramatic style, though still expressed in traditional metres, is a testimony to his deep concern for the people's sorrows. It was he who composed the Turkish national anthem after Mustafa Kemal Atatürk's victory, but soon afterward he left the country, disappointed with the religious policies of the Kemalists.

Atatürk's struggle for freedom also marks the real beginning of modern Turkish literature. The mainstream of novels, stories, and poems written during the 19th century had been replete with tears, world-weariness, and pessimism, but a postwar novel, *Ateşten gömlek*

Kemal Atatürk modernized Turkey's legal and educational systems. He also encouraged the adoption of a European way of life and the writing of Turkish in

("The Fire Shirt"), written by a woman, Halide Edib Adıvar (died 1964), reflected the brave new self-awareness of the Turkish nation. Some successful short stories about village life came from the pen of Ömer Seyfeddin (died 1920). The most-gifted interpreter and harshest critic of Turkey's social structure was Sabahattin Ali, who was murdered during a flight to Bulgaria in 1948. His major theme was the tragedy of the lower classes, and his writing is characterized by the same merciless realism that was later to be a feature of stories by many left-wing writers throughout the Islamic world. The "great old man of Turkish prose," Yakup Kadri Karaosmanoğlu (died 1974), displayed profound psychological insight, whether ironically describing the lascivious life in a Bektashi (Muslim mystic order) centre or a stranger's tragedy in an Anatolian village. Most of the Turkish novelists of the 1920s and '30s concentrated on the problems of becoming a modern nation, and in particular they reinterpreted the role of women in a liberated society.

Literary energies were set completely free in 1928, when Atatürk introduced the Latin alphabet, hoping that his people would forget their Islamic past along with the Arabic letters. From this time onward, especially after the language reform that was meant to rediscover the pre-Islamic roots of the Turkish language, Turkish literature followed the pattern of Western literature in all major respects, though with local overtones. Poets experimented with new forms and new topics. They discovered the significance of the Anatolian village, neglected—even forgotten—during the Ottoman period. Freeing themselves from the traditional rules of Persian poetry, they adopted simpler forms from Europe. In some cases the skillful blending of inherited Ottoman grace and borrowed French lyricism produced outstandingly beautiful poems, such as those of Ahmed Haşim (died 1933) and of Yahya Kemal Beyatlı (died 1958), in which the twilight world of old Istanbul is mirrored in soft evocative hues and melodious words. At the same time, the figure of Nazım Hikmet (died 1963) looms large in Turkish poetry. Expressing his progressive social attitude in truly poetical form, he used free rhythmical patterns quite brilliantly to enrapture his readers. His style, as well as his powerful, unforgettable images, has deeply influenced not only Turkish verse but also progressive Urdu and Persian poetry from the 1930s onward.

Persian Literatures

In Iran the situation resembled that in Turkey to a certain extent. While the last "classical" poet, Qāʾānī (died 1854), had been displaying the traditional glamorous artistry, his contemporary, the satirist Yaghmā (died 1859), had been using popular and comprehensible language to make coarse criticisms of contemporary society. As in the other Islamic countries, a move toward simplicity is discernible during the last decades of the 19th century. The members of the polytechnic college Dār ol-Fonūn (founded 1851), led by its erudite principal Reẕā Qolī Khān Hedāyat, helped to shape the "new" style by making translations from European languages. Nāṣer al-Dīn Shāh described his journeys to Europe in the late 1870s in a simple, unassuming style and in so doing set an example for future prose writers.

At the turn of the century, literature became for many younger writers an instrument of modernization and of revolution in the largest sense of the word. No longer did they want to complain, in inherited fixed forms, of some boy whose face was like the moon. Instead, the feelings and situation of women were stated and interpreted. Their oppression, their problems, and their grievances are a major theme of literature in this transition period of the first decades of the 20th century. The "King of Poets," Muḥammad Taqī Bahār (died 1951), who had been actively working before World War I for democracy, now devoted himself to a variety of cultural activities, but his poems, though highly classical in form, were of great influence; they dealt with contemporary events and appealed to a wide public.

One branch of modern Persian literature is closely connected with a group of Persian authors who lived in Berlin after World War I. There they established the Kaviani Press (named after a mythical blacksmith called Kaveh, who had saved the Iranian kingdom), and among the poems they printed were several by ʿĀref Qazvīnī (died 1934), one of the first truly modern writers. They also published the first short stories of Muhammad ʿAli Jamalzadah (died 1997), whose outspoken social criticism and complete break with the traditional inflated and pompous prose style inaugurated a new era of modern Persian prose. Many young writers adopted this new form, among them Sadeq Hedayat (died 1951), whose stories—written entirely in a direct everyday language with a purity of expression that was an artistic achievement—have been translated into many languages. They reflect the sufferings of living individuals; instead of dealing in literary clichés, they describe the distress and anxiety of a hopeless youth. The influence of Franz Kafka (some of whose work Hedayat translated) is perceptible in his writing, and he has a tendency toward psychological probing shared by many Persian writers.

As in neighbouring countries, women played a considerable role in the development of modern Persian literature. The lyrics of Parvīn Eʿteṣāmī (died 1940) are regarded as near classics, despite a trace of sentimentality in their sympathetic treatment of the poor. Some Persian writers whose left-wing political ideas brought them into conflict with the government left for what is now Tajikistan. Of these, the gifted poet Abū al-Qāsim Lāhūtī (died 1957) is their most important representative.

A poet and philosopher, Muḥammad Iqbāl is also known for his influential efforts to direct his fellow Muslims in British-ruled India toward the establishment of a separate Muslim state.

India: Urdu and Persian

Persian literature in the Indian subcontinent did not have such importance as in earlier centuries, for English replaced Persian as the official language in 1835. Nevertheless, there were some outstanding poets who excelled in Urdu. One of them was Mīrzā Asadullāh Khān Ghālib (died 1869), the undisputed master of Urdu lyrics. He regarded himself, however, as the leading authority on high Persian style and was an accomplished writer of Persian prose and poetry. But much more important was a later poet, Sir Muḥammad Iqbāl (died 1938), who chose Persian to convey his message not only to the peoples of Muslim India but also to Afghans and Persians. Reinterpreting many of the old mystical ideas in the light of modern teachings, he taught the quiescent Muslim peoples self-awareness, urging them to develop their personalities to achieve true individualism. His first *mas̄navī*, called *Asrār-e khudī* (1915; "Secrets of the Self"), deeply shocked all those who enjoyed the dreamlike sweetness of most traditional Persian poetry. One of his later Persian works, *Payām-e Mashriq* (1923; "Message of the East"), is an effective answer to Goethe's *Poems of the East and West* (1819). In the *Jāvīd-nāmeh* (1932; "The Song of Eternity") he poetically elaborated the old topic of the "heavenly journey," discussing with the inhabitants of the spheres a variety of political, social, and religious problems. Iqbāl's approach is unique. Although he used the conventional literary forms and leaned heavily on the inspiration of Jalāl al-Dīn al-Rūmī, he must be considered one of the select few poets of modern Islam who, because of their honesty and their capacity for expressing their message in memorable poetic form, appeal to many readers outside the Muslim world.

Chapter 8

The Modern Period

The modern period of Islamic literatures can be said to begin after World War II. The topics discussed before then still appeared, but outspoken social criticism became an even more important feature. Literature was no longer a leisurely pastime for members of the upper classes. Writers born in the villages and from non-privileged classes began to win literary fame through their firsthand knowledge of social problems. Many writers started their careers as journalists, developing a literary style that retained the immediacy of journalistic observation.

Prose

During the middle decades of the 20th century and beyond, young left-wing writers in Iraq and Syria shared the critical and aggressive attitudes of their contemporaries in Turkey and Egypt and took positions on all political issues. Most of them responded to the works of Bertolt Brecht and Karl Marx. Freudian influence could be detected in many modern short stories or novels in the Islamic countries. In the Middle East the existentialist philosophy gained many followers who tried to reflect its interpretation of life in their literary works. In fact, almost every current of modern Western philosophy and psychology, every artistic trend and attitude, was eagerly adopted at some point by young Arab, Turkish, or Persian writers during the period after World War II.

Arabic Literature

In Egypt a great change in literary preoccupations came about after 1952. The name of Naguib Mahfouz (died 2006) is of particular importance. He was at first a novelist mainly concerned with the lower middle classes (his outstanding work is a trilogy dealing with the life of a Cairo family), but afterward he turned to socially committed literature, using all the techniques of modern fiction—of which he is the undisputed master in Arabic. In 1988 he became the first Arabic writer to receive the Nobel Prize for Literature. Mahfouz was probably the single most important figure in the genre's widespread acceptance.

The problems facing poor and destitute villagers is the subject treated in ʿAbd al-Raḥmān al-Sharqāwī's novel *Al-Arḍ* (1954; *Egyptian Earth*), another important novel from Egypt. While the novel now flourishes throughout the Arab world, the demands of time and expense in both creation and publication may make it somewhat less plentiful than the short story. A major advance in short-story writing occurred in the early and mid-20th century with a group of Egyptian writers who became known as Jamāʿat al-Madrasah Ḥadīthah ("New School Group").

While Egyptian writers continued to advance the generic prominence of the short story, writers in other regions—albeit with differing chronologies—developed their own local traditions; these include the Palestinian Khalīl Baydas, the Tunisian ʿAlī al-Duʿājī, the Iraqi Dhū al-Nūn Ayyūb, and the Lebanese Tawfīq Yūsuf ʿAwwād. With the increasing emergence of women into the public domain (once again a variable phenomenon across countries), women writers began

The novels of Naguib Mahfouz, which were among the first to gain widespread acceptance in the Arabic-speaking world, brought the genre to maturity within Arabic literature.

to contribute short stories that provided new insights into issues of family and society; among such pioneers are Suhayr al-Qalamāwī of Egypt, Ulfat Idilbī of Syria, and Samīrah ʿAzzām of Palestine.

Two writers, by their concentration on the art of the short story, have come to be widely acknowledged as genuine masters of their craft: Yūsuf Idrīs of Egypt and Zakariyyā Tāmir of Syria. Beginning a writing career in the 1950s with an outpouring of story collections, Idrīs—who wrote plays and novels, as well as publishing many more story collections in the last half of the 20th century—managed to recount in his vignettes the realities of the life of the poor, primarily in the Egyptian countryside but also in the ancient quarters of Cairo. As political oppression began to impinge upon the daily life of Egyptians, Idrīs added to his authentic visions a series of new and symbolic portrayals of oppression and alienation that encapsulated an entire era in contemporary Arab societies. Tāmir's contributions to the genre tend to be concerned with a highly terse and symbolic representation of the callous indifference of authority and bureaucracy, often expressed through nightmarish visions of violence, both verbal and physical.

At the beginning of the 21st century, the short story was by far the most popular literary genre in the Arab world; for nonprofessional writers it was a relatively short-term project with the prospect of many publication outlets, and for readers it provided an opportunity to interpret a brief expression of contemporary concerns, both social and political. The short story was also on frequent occasions readily adaptable to the more lucrative and increasingly available alternatives of film and television. A very short list of distinguished contributors to the genre would include Aḥmad Būzufūr (Būzfūr) of Morocco, Ḥasan Naṣr of Tunisia, Ḥaydar Ḥaydar of Syria, Fuʾād al-Tikirlī and Muḥammad Khuḍayyir of Iraq, Laylā al-ʿUthmān of Kuwait, and Yaḥyā al-Ṭāhir ʿAbdallāh, Muḥammad al-Bisāṭī, Salwā Bakr, and Ibrāhīm Aṣlān of Egypt.

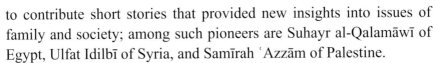

Turkey

As literacy spread to the countryside after the founding of the Turkish republic in 1923 and the output of urban writers became more varied, Turkish writers expanded their thematic horizons. Among the most influential novelists of the generation born in the 1920s is Yashar Kemal. Born in a small village in southeastern Anatolia, where he never completed his secondary education, Kemal arrived in Istanbul in 1951 and found work with the prestigious newspaper *Cumhuriyet*. In 1955 he published the novella *Teneke* ("The Tin Pan") and his first full-length novel, *İnce Memed* ("Thin Memed"; Eng. trans. *Memed, My Hawk*), both of which brought him immediate recognition in Turkey. The latter, like many of his other novels and short stories, is set in the rural eastern Anatolia of his youth and portrays the glaring social contradictions there, often aggravated by the process of modernization under the capitalist system. While Kemal's works appear to be realistic and straightforward, his subtle narrative techniques ensure that his works are appreciated by a wide range of readers.

Fellow Turkish novelist Adalet Ağaoğlu portrayed life from a more personal and introverted perspective. Her novels deal with a broad spectrum of the social changes that occurred within the Turkish republic, and she was among the first Turkish writers to treat sexual themes in depth. Beginning with *Troya'da olüm vardı* (1963; *Death in Troy*), Bilge Karasu created works that display a sophisticated narrative style. Although he wrote prolifically in every genre, Necati Cumalı is known primarily as a short-story writer.

The two best-known novelists in Turkey at the turn of the 21st century were Orhan Pamuk (who won the Nobel Prize for Literature

ORHAN PAMUK

The Turkish novelist Orhan Pamuk is best known for works that probe Turkish identity and history. Born in Istanbul in 1952, Pamuk was raised in a wealthy and Western-oriented family. He began writing seriously in 1974 and eight years later published his first novel, *Cevdet Bey ve oğulları* ("Cevdet Bey and His Sons"), a sweeping history of an Istanbul family during and after the establishment of the Turkish republic. He followed it with *Sessiz ev* (1983; *Silent House*), relying on multiple narrators to shape the story of a family gathering on the eve of the Turkish military coup of 1980. Pamuk first achieved international fame with *Beyaz kale* (1985; *The White Castle*), his third novel, which explores the nature of identity through the story of a learned young Italian captured and made a slave to a scholar in 17th-century Istanbul. His subsequent novels, which were widely translated, include *Kara kitap* (1990;*The Black Book*), a dense depiction of Istanbul, and the mysteries *Yeni hayat* (1996; *The New Life*) and *Benim adım kırmızı* (1998; *My Name Is Red*).

In *Kar* (2002; *Snow*) a Turkish poet living in exile in Germany faces the tensions between East and West when he travels to a poor town in a remote area of Turkey. *Masumiyet müzesi* (2008; *The Museum of Innocence*) investigates the relationship between an older man and his second cousin. Thwarted in his attempts to marry her, the man begins to collect objects that she has touched. Pamuk replicated the titular museum in reality, using a house in Istanbul to display a range of items amassed while plotting the story; it opened to the public in 2012, accompanied by the catalogue *Şeylerin masumiyeti* (*The Innocence of Objects*). Among Pamuk's other works are *İstanbul: hatıralar ve şehir* (2004; *Istanbul: Memories and the City*, also published as *Istanbul: Memories of a City*), a partly fictionalized memoir, and *The Naive and Sentimental*

(continued on the next page)

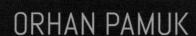

(continued from the previous page)

Novelist (2010), in which he explicated his theories on the novel as a literary form. *Kafamda Bir Tuhaflık* (2014; *A Strangeness in My Mind*) is a love story set in Istanbul.

in 2006) and Latife Tekin. In distinct ways, both expanded the scope of the novel in Turkish and opened up modern Turkish literature to readers in Europe and North America. To a large extent, their differences in social background and gender impelled them toward radically divergent literary paths. Many of Pamuk's novels, often autobiographical and intricately plotted, show an understanding of traditional Turkish Islamic culture tempered by a belief that Turkey's future lies in the West. Tekin's deconstruction of narrative duplicates the deconstruction of every element of the life of the former villagers, which does not spare any part of their former religious and social belief system. The manner in which her novels use the Turkish language sets her critique of modernity apart from and beyond earlier attempts to treat similar themes in Turkish literature.

Iran

After Reza Shah's fall in 1941, when for a short time there was greater freedom of the press in Iran, another generation of prose writers emerged, the most prominent representatives of which were Sadeq Chubak, a clever writer whose short stories show the influence of the American novelist Ernest Hemingway, and Jalal Al-e Ahmad, whose long essay *Gharbzadegī* (1962; "Westoxication") became widely influential as an indictment of the slavish imitation of the West in Iranian society under the Pahlavi regime. Simin Daneshvar, his wife, had much success with her novel *Savūshūn* (1969; "The Sacrifice";

Eng. trans. *A Persian Requiem*, or *Savushun*), which describes the disruption of traditional society by foreign occupation during World War II. Among prose writers of the later 20th century, the influence of modern narrative techniques, inspired by Western writers such as James Joyce and William Faulkner, was strong, particularly in the works of Hushang Golshiri. His depiction of the decay of the ancient Iranian aristocracy in *Shāzdeh Eḥtejāb* (1968; "Prince Iḥtijāb"; Eng. trans. *The Prince*), a short novel that was also made into a film, is one of many instances of the symbiosis of literature and the visual and performing arts in modern Persian literature. A symbiosis of the arts also marks the work of Ghulam Husayn Saʿidi (Gholam-Hossein Saʿedi), who wrote short stories as well as plays for the theatre and scripts for Iranian films.

The participation of women writers in modern literature increased considerably during the second half of the 20th century. Best known outside Iran is Shahrnoush Parsipour's novella *Zanān bidūn-i mardān* (1978; *Women Without Men*), which recounts the attempts of five women to overcome the limitations put upon their lives by male dominance in a traditional society. Like many other contemporary Iranian writers, Parsipour uses the narrative technique of magic realism in imitation of such Latin American authors as Gabriel García Márquez. In contrast to the late-20th-century tendency by writers to apply modern narrative techniques to their novels stands the social realism of Mahmoud Dawlatabadi. His great novel *Kalīdar*, published in 10 parts (1978–84), depicts the lives of nomads in the plains of Khorāsān, the author's native region.

POETRY

The new attitudes that informed literature after World War II became even more conspicuous in poetry than in prose. Helped in part by

French and English literary influences, Arabic poetry broke from classical tradition, a profound shift that also had its roots in efforts by nations across the Middle East to gain independence. The creation of the State of Israel also influenced the meaning and purpose of Arabic poetry. T.S. Eliot's poetry and criticism were influential in dethroning the Romanticism that many poets had adopted in the 1920s and '30s. One of the first and most important attempts at creating a modern Arabic poetic diction was made in the late 1940s by the Iraqi poet and critic Nāzik al-Malāʾikah (died 2007), whose poems, in free but rhyming verse, gave substance to the shadow of her melancholia. Free rhythm and a colourful imagination distinguished the best poems of the younger Arabs: even when their poems did not succeed, their experimentation, their striving for sincerity, their burning quest for identity, their rebellion against social injustice, could be readily perceived. Indeed, one of the most noticeable aspects of contemporary Arabic poetry written during the second half of the 20th century was its political engagement, evident in the poems of Palestinian writers such as Mahmoud Darwish (died 2008), whose verses once more prove the strength, expressiveness, and vitality of the Arabic language. The Iraqi modernist poet ʿAbd al-Wahhāb al-Bayātī (died 1999) combined political engagement with lyrical mysticism. Others, without withdrawing into a world of uncommitted dreams, managed to create in their poetry an atmosphere that broke up the harsh light of reality into its colourful components. Poets such as the Lebanese Adonis and Tawfīq al-Ṣāʾigh, or the Egyptian dramatist Ṣalāḥ ʿAbd al-Ṣabur, made use of traditional imagery in a new, sometimes esoteric, often fascinating and daring way.

Almost the same situation developed in Iran. One notable poet was Forugh Farrokhzad, who wrote powerful and feminine poetry. Her free verses, interpreting the insecurities of the age, are full of longing; though often bitter, they are truly poetic. Poems by such critically minded writers as Seyāvūsh Kasrāʾī also borrow the classical heritage of poetic imagery, transforming it into expressions that win a response from modern readers. After 1979, many writers in the Islamic Republic of Iran felt the pinch of censorship, and much literary activity was curtailed.

In Turkey the adoption of Western forms began in the 1920s. Of major importance in modern Turkish literature was Orhan Veli Kanık (died 1950), who combined perfect technique with "Istanbulian" charm. His work is sometimes melancholy, sometimes frivolous, but always convincing. He strongly influenced a group of poets connected with the avant-garde literary magazine *Varlik* ("Existence"). The powerful poetry of the leftist writer Nazım Hikmet (died 1963) influenced progressive poets all over the Muslim world; Ataol Behramoğlu was often considered Hikmet's successor. Fazıl Hüsnü Dağlarca was another poet with leftist views. His modernist poetry made him one of Turkey's most influential poets during the post-World War II era. The poetry of Hilmi Yavuz melded the aesthetics of Ottoman civilization with modernist poetic forms. His interweaving of past and present was typical of many Turkish poets in the last decades of the 20th century.

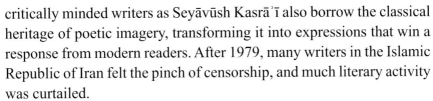

CONCLUSION

The Western world has rarely given Islamic literature the attention and respect that it deserves. By the end of the Middle Ages, Islamic motives wandered into the belles lettres of Europe, and Islamic scientific books formed a basis for the development of Western science. Islamic culture as such, however, was rather an object of hatred than of admiration. A more objective appreciation of both the works of art and of literature did not start until the mid-17th century, when the first works from Persian literature were translated, influencing German classical literature. A bias against the cultures of the East persisted, however, until after the 18th-century Age of Enlightenment. The indefatigable work of the British scholars at Fort William at Calcutta (now Kolkata) brought new literary treasures to Europe, where they were studied carefully by specialists in the emerging field of Islamic studies. Poets such as Goethe in Germany in the early 19th century paved the way for a deeper understanding of Islamic poetry. Islamic literatures, however, continue to be known to the larger Western public almost exclusively by *The Thousand and One Nights* (translated first in the early 18th century), Omar Khayyam's *robāʿiyyāt*, and the lyrics of Ḥāfeẓ. Even experts who were aware of the immense wealth of the literatures in the different Islamic languages (such as Arabic, Persian, Turkish, and Urdu) until the 20th century rarely appreciated the literatures from an aesthetic viewpoint; rather, they used them as a source for lexicography and for philological and historical research.

In the 21st century, Islamic literature is increasingly accessible to Western audiences. While there is much that has not been translated, an ever-growing number of works now exist in translation. Opportunities to learn the languages these works were written in and read them in the original have grown, too. From a poem over a thousand years old or a short story from the last decade, there is a real wealth of literature to be explored.

GLOSSARY

ALLITERATION The repetition of consonant sounds at the beginning of words or stressed syllables.

APHORISM A concise expression of doctrine or principle or any generally accepted truth conveyed in a pithy, memorable statement.

ASSONANCE The repetition of stressed vowel sounds within words with different end consonants, as in the phrase "quite like."

BELLES LETTRES Literature that is an end in itself and is not practical or purely informative. The term can refer generally to poetry, fiction, drama, etc., or more specifically to light, entertaining, sophisticated literature.

CONCEIT A figure of speech, usually a simile or metaphor, that forms an extremely ingenious or fanciful parallel between apparently dissimilar or incongruous objects or situations.

COSMOGRAPHY A general description of the world or of the universe.

DEVICE Something (as a figure of speech) in a literary work designed to achieve a particular artistic effect.

ELEGY A meditative lyric poem lamenting the death of a public personage or of a friend or loved one; by extension, any reflective lyric on the broader theme of human mortality.

HEMISTICH Half a poetic line, usually divided by a pause that is called a caesura.

HETERODOX Holding or expressing unorthodox beliefs or opinions.

KŪFIC The earliest extant Islamic script (style of handwritten alphabet). It was used by early Muslims to record the Qurʾān.

LYRICISM An intense personal style or quality in an art (as poetry).

MAGIC REALISM A narrative strategy characterized by the matter-of-fact inclusion of fantastic or mythical elements into seemingly realistic fiction; it is most common in Latin American literature.

METRE The rhythmic pattern of a poetic line.

PANEGYRIC A formal speech or writing eulogizing someone or something.

PHILOLOGY The study of the history of language, including the historical study of literary texts.

PROSODY The study of all the elements of language that contribute toward acoustic and rhythmic effects, chiefly in poetry but also in prose.

RHETORIC The study of the principles and rules of composition.

SATIRE An artistic form, chiefly literary and dramatic, in which human or individual vices, follies, abuses, or shortcomings are held up to censure by means of ridicule, derision, burlesque, irony, parody, caricature, or other methods, sometimes with an intent to inspire social reform.

SHĪʿITE Relating to one of the two major branches of Islam, the branch of Islam comprising sects believing in Ali and the Imams as the only rightful successors of Muhammad and in the concealment and messianic return of the last recognized Imam.

STROPHIC Relating to verses, particularly to a group that form a distinct unit within a poem.

SUFISM Mystical Islamic belief and practice in which Muslims seek to find the truth of divine love and knowledge through direct personal experience of God.

SUNNI Relating to one of the two major branches of Islam, the branch that consists of the majority of that religion's adherents. Sunni Muslims regard their sect as the mainstream and traditionalist branch of Islam, as distinguished from the minority sect, the Shīʿites.

TROPE A word, phrase, or image used in a new and different way in order to create an artistic effect.

BIBLIOGRAPHY

Arabic Literature

Comprehensive overviews of Arabic literature include Roger Allen, *The Arabic Literary Heritage: The Development of Its Genres and Criticism* (1998), and *An Introduction to Arabic Literature* (2000); M.M. Badawi, *A Short History of Modern Arabic Literature* (1993); Pierre Cachia, *Arabic Literature: An Overview* (2002); Julie Scott Meisami and Paul Starkey (eds.), *Encyclopedia of Arabic Literature,* 2 vol. (1998); A.F.L. Beeston et al. (eds.), *Arabic Literature to the End of the Umayyad Period* (1983); Robin Ostle (ed.), *Modern Literature in the Near and Middle East, 1850–1970* (1991); M.J.L. Young, J.D. Latham, and R.B. Serjeant (eds.), *Religion, Learning, and Science in the ʿAbbasid Period* (1991); M.M. Badawi (ed.), *Modern Arabic Literature* (1992); Gregor Schoeler, *The Oral and the Written in Early Islam*, trans. by Uwe Vagelpohl, ed. by James E. Montgomery (2006; originally published in French, 2002); Andras Hamori, *On the Art of Medieval Arabic Literature* (1974); Reynold A. Nicholson, *A Literary History of the Arabs* (1907, reissued 1998); and Paul Starkey, *Modern Arabic Literature* (2006).

Three authoritative collections of essays in the series *The Cambridge History of Arabic Literature* (1983–2006) are Julia Ashtiany et al. (eds.), *ʿAbbasid Belles-Lettres* (1990); Maria Rosa Menocal, Raymond P. Scheindlin, and Michael Sells (eds.), *The Literature of Al-Andalus* (2000); and Roger Allen and D.S. Richards (eds.), *Arabic Literature in the Post-Classical Period* (2006).

Persian Literature

Edward G. Browne, *A Literary History of Persia*, 4 vol. (1902–24, reissued 1999), although obsolescent, still provides a very readable introduction to Persian literature and includes many texts in translation.

Ehsan Yarshater (ed.), *Encyclopaedia Iranica* (1982–), is the most important reference work for Persian literature. A.J. Arberry, *Classical Persian Literature* (1958, reissued 1994), covers the "golden period" from the 9th century to the end of the 15th and to some extent updates Browne's monumental work. Jan Rypka, *History of Iranian Literature,* ed. by Karl Jahn (1968; originally published in Czech, 1956), authoritatively surveys modern literary scholarship in Iran, the West, and eastern Europe and includes chapters on the ancient and modern literatures of Iran, the Indian subcontinent, and Central Asia, but it provides no original texts. Ehsan Yarshater (ed.), *Persian Literature* (1988), is a volume of essays by several authors on aspects of classical and modern Persian literature.

The prosody of classical poetry is treated in L.P. Elwell-Sutton, *The Persian Metre*s (1976); and Finn Thiesen, *A Manual of Classical Persian Prosody* (1982). Annemarie Schimmel, *A Two-Colored Brocad*e (1992; originally published in German, 1984), examines imagery in Persian poetry. Other studies of Persian poetry are Julie Scott Meisami, *Medieval Persian Court Poetry* (1987); and J.T.P. de Bruijn, *Persian Sufi Poetry* (1997). Julie Scott Meisami, *Persian Historiography to the End of the Twelfth Century* (1999), surveys early historical writing in Persian.

Edward G. Browne, *The Press and Poetry of Modern Persia* (1914, reprinted 1983), gives a firsthand account of literary events during the Constitutional Revolution of 1906. H. Kamshad, *Modern Persian Prose Literatur*e (1966, reissued 1996), focuses especially on the work of Sadeq Hedayat. Ahmad Karimi-Hakkak, *Recasting Persian Poetry: Scenarios of Poetic Modernity in Iran* (1995), studies the change of poetical paradigm that took place in the late 19th and early 20th centuries. Aspects of modern poetry and prose are investigated in M.R. Ghanoonparvar, *Prophets of Doom: Literature as a Socio-Political Phenomenon in Modern Iran* (1984), and *In a Persian Mirror: Images of the West and Westerners in Iranian Fiction* (1993).

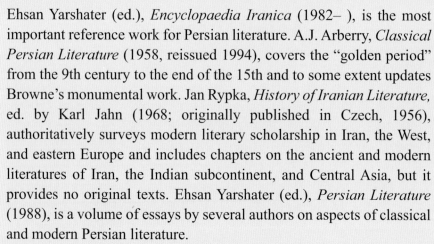

TURKISH LITERATURE

İhsan Işik, *Encyclopedia of Turkish Authors*, 3 vol. (2005; originally published in Turkish, 2004), provides comprehensive coverage of Turkish authors through the ages. Karl Reichl, *Turkic Oral Epic Poetry: Tradition, Forms, Poetic Structure* (1992), is the best introduction to the epics of the Turkic peoples.

E.J.W. Gibb, *A History of Ottoman Poetry*, 6 vol. (1900–09, reprinted 1963–84), is the standard history. While based primarily on critics of the late Ottoman period, it had not been entirely superseded even at the turn of the 21st century. Walter G. Andrews, *An Introduction to Ottoman Poetry* (1976), and *Poetry's Voice, Society's Song: Ottoman Lyric Poetry* (1985), examine both the formal properties of Ottoman poetry and its social context.

Among the few critical treatments in English of modern Turkish literature is Ahmet Ö. Evin, *Origins and Development of the Turkish Novel* (1983). Louis Mitler, *Contemporary Turkish Writers: A Critical Bio-Bibliography of Leading Writers in the Turkish Republican Period Up to 1980* (1988), is a useful starting point for scholarship produced during and before the 1980s. Kenan Çayır, *Islamic Literature in Contemporary Turkey: From Epic to Novel* (2007), discusses issues in modern Turkish literature.

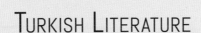

INDEX